Solomon on Leadership

Leadership Maxims from a king.

The wisdom paradigm of leadership; second in the life coaching series based on the Proverbs of Solomon.

For leadership hopefuls of all faiths and persuasion.

by Pilgrim Sojourner

I0479268

Table of Contents

Dedication

This book is dedicated to those who have endured the tyranny of despotic management enamored with self-serving aggrandizement, their own importance, image, and autocratic power.

Copyrights

With Gratitude and Thanksgiving

I pray the LORD's Spirit has hovered over and attended this work and its final rendering has not altered or distorted His message; that the Word of God has been accurately handled.

Acknowledgements

I am deeply grateful for the free, on-line availability of the Blue Letter Bible and the Bible Hub. These resources have been invaluable and are highly recommended to anyone seeking Bible study tools and information. Please consider providing your financial support to preserve the availability at no charge to users.

Disclaimer-Reader Alert

This is a work of personal experience and observation; no clinical claim is made or implied. Views expressed are my own based on circumstance that has shaped and reshaped my thinking over time and has made me, more profoundly and prophetically, understand everything in life has intent; there is Divine purpose in everything, that [28]... *all things work together for good to those who love God, to those who are called according to his purpose. Romans 8 [KJV]*

Introduction

In the main, positions of power are vigorously pursued by the self-serving, ruddered by obsession with the perks tethered to the role. They covet front of the line privilege with the advantages of wealth, connection, influence, and the recognition we see in religious rulers, familial dynasties, regals, presidents, prime ministers, military authorities, dictators, and tyrants.

Leadership, when desired as service, is a noble pursuit.

To a small, rather more exclusive group, leadership embodies the quality of shepherding that seeks to blend goals, objectives, and vision with the life aspirations and aims of those within their sphere of control.

These authority seekers are energized by the need to propel actions that shape controllable circumstances in ways that best offer the widest berth of opportunity and the pursuit of excellence not only for themselves, but also for those in their charge.

The shepherding leader embraces the lead by example model because of its testimony and power; when conduct adheres to unwavering trustable standards there is surety and security. They understand:

- Truth, trust, and transparency are character essentials.

- Effective leaders strive to influence motives and thinking in others, a kinship of ideas fuses in cause and vision.

- Even the best leaders make wrongful decisions that wound.

- Considering the advice and input from others are components of good decision making, but responsibility for outcomes always rests with leadership.

- Accountability is a step-up quality that is exampled.

- Promoting unwise, damaging courses of action that are policy imposed is a mark of character and intellectual weakness.

- Equity is never achieved through punitive actions applied to everyone for the misdeeds of a few.

- Doing the wrong thing, even exceptionally well, is of no value.

- Connection and position often afford the inane, uninformed, and unworthy a place at the table.

- Subordinating personality likes and dislikes is part of the job.

Leadership Maxims

Leadership skills are almost never acquired through textbook study or classroom instruction. The attributes, qualities, and core values of effective leadership are best learned and put into practice when leader hopefuls are mentored or otherwise exposed to proven leader talent.

For the Record...

In my professional career I have yet to be in an environment that inspired me to believe in a vision and voluntarily follow. Just dummy-up and do what you are told was consistently the message.

Bosses to whom I have been subjected have been propelled by a motivation to climb the success ladder stepping on, or over, those considered impediments or unworthy of merit, and some by an evil craving to hurt others.

Hard experience has taught me it's about spin, lies, character assassination grounded in personality preferences or back-biting gossip, marginalization, belittlement, bullying, and disciplinary sessions driven by a bruised ego where the "crime" did not fit the punishment.

Most often character traits of self-preservation without risk taking, naked favoritism, platitudes that are never backed by action, plagiarizing the ideas of others, and taking credit for solutions not their own are the behaviors served up with stunning regularity. Lip service to the importance of people as the most valued resource is programed in. Sadly, the walk and the talk are at opposite ends of the spectrum.

This book is a critical examination of leadership qualities and characteristics. The motives, core values, character development, practice, and source of wisdom that inspire and shape effective shepherding, servant leaders. My hope: it will stimulate and propel change that promotes behavior modification in leader aspirants.
Pilgrim Sojourner
December 25, 2023

The Proverbs

Solomon wrote some three-thousand proverbs and collected many more. His uncanny ability to read people and events is legendary. When used as a daily devotional and life coaching tool the *Proverbs* offer valuable insights for gaining the wisdom that informs choices. Repetitive themes of righteousness, most often denoted wisdom, prudence, justice, equity, and discretion contrast sharply with wickedness typified as simple minded, evil, foolish, scoffers, perverse, devious, or indolent.

With all his strengths, weaknesses, foibles, and flaws Solomon is real. We gain an unshakeable confidence from knowing Scripture paints God's vessels as they lived, defects and all; people to whom we can readily relate. My prayer, you will be inspired through his words and draw assurance from his person.

Wisdom

Wisdom, Solomon counsels *4:7...is] the principal thing; [Therefore] get wisdom."* Pursue wisdom because by it all other choices are made. Let this mind-set shape and control your deepest desires. Pray for, cultivate, practice, and hone qualities of discernment, understanding, discretion, insight, prudence, and justice.

The Wise

Biblical text teaches us the wise are not wretched victims of unfolding circumstances; they do not see themselves in a fog of confusion, victimized by those around them; they do not suffer prolonged sessions of hand wringing and unknowing. They understand themselves not merely as a product of genetic inheritance and environmental conditioning, but as a vessel made by God, in His image Who works *13...in you both to will and to do for His good pleasure. Philippines 2*

The wise exercise control over choices in matters of personal and professional deportment, sexual conduct, mate selection and marriage, home life and child rearing. Truth, owning responsibility in financial affairs, providing for the poor, and choosing civil authorities to lead in government are understood as core values that form behavioral standards.

Life is seen as a journey continuously honing practices of self-awareness and self-control, exercising discretion, distancing oneself from evil, and diligent study that elevates our understanding of the Word in grateful obedience to our Lord.

Proverbs 1

¹The proverbs of Solomon, son of David, king of Israel: ²To know wisdom and instruction, to understand words of insight, ³to receive instruction in wise dealing, in righteousness, justice, and equity; ⁴to give prudence to the simple, knowledge and discretion to the youth—

⁵Let the wise hear and increase in learning, and the one who understands obtain guidance, ⁶to understand a proverb and a saying, the words of the wise and their riddles.
⁷The fear of the LORD is the beginning of knowledge; fools despise wisdom and instruction. ⁸Hear, my son, your father's instruction, and forsake not your mother's teaching, ⁹for they are a graceful garland for your head and pendants for your neck.

¹⁰My son, if sinners entice you, do not consent. ¹¹If they say, "Come with us, let us lie in wait for blood; let us ambush the innocent without reason; ¹²like Sheol let us swallow them alive, and whole, like those who go down to the pit; ¹³we shall find all precious goods, we shall fill our houses with plunder; ¹⁴throw in your lot among us; we will all have one purse"-- ¹⁵my son, do not walk in the way with them; hold back your foot from their paths, ¹⁶for their feet run to evil, and they make haste to shed blood. ¹⁷For in vain is a net spread in the sight of any bird, ¹⁸but these men lie in wait for their own blood; they set an ambush for their own lives. ¹⁹Such are the ways of everyone who is greedy for unjust gain; it takes away the life of its possessors.

²⁰Wisdom cries aloud in the street, in the markets she raises her voice; ²¹at the head of the noisy streets she cries out; at the entrance of the city gates she speaks: ²²"How long, O simple ones, will you love being simple? How long will scoffers delight in their scoffing and fools hate knowledge? ²³If you turn at my reproof, behold, I will pour out my spirit to you; I will make my words known to you. ²⁴Because I have called and you refused to listen, have stretched out my hand and no one

has heeded, 25because you have ignored all my counsel and would have none of my reproof, 26I also will laugh at your calamity; I will mock when terror strikes you, 27when terror strikes you like a storm and your calamity comes like a whirlwind, when distress and anguish come upon you. 28Then they will call upon me, but I will not answer; they will seek me diligently but will not find me. 29Because they hated knowledge and did not choose the fear of the LORD, 30would have none of my counsel and despised all my reproof, 31therefore they shall eat the fruit of their way, and have their fill of their own devices. 32For the simple are killed by their turning away, and the complacency of fools destroys them; 33but whoever listens to me will dwell secure and will be at ease, without dread of disaster." [ESV]

Bio-Shorts

We can choose to be inspired by those that have preceded us. We have the power of choice, to be advised and instructed by the best parts of surviving examples.

Jesus the Christ- Son of God, King of Kings, Lord of Lords, Savior of humankind.

Christ, we are taught in the Scripture, set aside His position in the triune Godhead in service to the Father. His earthly mission changed the course of human history. His ministry birthed the Christian religion.

He was a model youngster, obedient to His earthly parents. As an adult His steadfast resolve for righteousness, calm demeaner and gentle treatment of others was exemplary. Continually thronged with crowds of needy people he was rarely afforded "me-time."

He stood before His accusers saying nothing; He was stripped, beaten to an unrecognizable state, and suffered crucifixion when He could have crushed His abusers with the breath of His mouth.

Having completed His substitutionary mission for sin and defeating death in resurrection He is now returned to heaven and will yet again be subject to the Father's redemptive timetable in His reappearance.

Leadership Maxim: The willingness to subordinate self-interests in favor of a greater good takes resolute, unwavering commitment. Our Lord is, and will remain, the most exalted model of servant leadership and power under control in human history. Learn of, and from Him, seek Him as you grow in life and your leadership role.

[i]**Joseph** - 11th son of the patriarch Jacob, grandson of Isaac, great grandson of Abraham; God blessed with enormous

talent, intelligence, and gifts of future-sight; convict, Egyptian vice-Pharoah.

Joseph was the preferred son in his family and his father's preference was no secret. Carelessly prone to boasting and recounting dreams in which family members bowed down to him, Joseph made himself despised. Overt favoritism and his crowing so provoked the jealousy and vicious hatred of his brothers that they hid him in a pit, sold him into slavery, and reported his death to their father.

He was taken to Egypt and there re-sold as a slave into the house of Potiphar, a well-placed official in Pharaoh's court. Owing to the great blessing of God he prospers and is raised to second in command of the household, but Potiphar had a wife with a roaming eye. Daily she pestered him and when she could not persuade him into intimacy charged him with rape.

Potiphar, inflamed by the report, ordered his immediate incarceration; but again, Joseph is favored by his captors and appointed custodian of prisoners. During his confinement Joseph interprets the dreams of two royal servants imprisoned with him. One man's dream foretells his death, the other predicts restoration of his position before Pharaoh.

Two full years pass and when Pharaoh is unsettled by his own troubling dreams the servant remembered Joseph. He is summoned, interprets Pharoah's dreams, and afterward rises to a position of authority second only to Pharaoh himself.

With the passage of time a widespread famine plagued the region. Joseph's brothers are driven to seek provisions in Egypt. Through a series of providential events his entire family is brought to Egypt and there the Hebrew nation is preserved until the exodus four centuries later.

Leadership Maxims: Adversity, when its lessons are rightly appropriated, is a means of tempering the will. Adapting to circumstance is the challenge, do not dwell on that which you have no power to change. Work around impediments and develop a problem-solving mentality. Waiting for and recognizing the right moment to act or speak is a patience building trial.

iiMoses- Levite, Hebrew profit, adopted son of Pharaoh's daughter, God's chosen man as leader of the Hebrew exodus from Egypt.

Born to Hebrew slave parents Moses was hidden for the first three months of his life owing to an Egyptian "final solution" aimed at Jewish infant boys. He was set adrift on the Nile and through a chain of divinely inspired events he came to be reared and educated in the house of Pharaoh.

At forty Prince Moses, heir apparent to the throne, took it into his head to visit *23his brethren, the sons of Israel [Acts 7]* to see for himself the plight of the people. As he passed among them, he witnessed an Egyptian beating an Hebrew. In a momentary response, he killed the Egyptian and hid his body in the sand. Fearing discovery and Pharaoh's anger he fled to the desert and was forty years more in the wilderness of Midian tending sheep for his father-in-law Jethro.

At the age of eighty, in spite of what may have been a speech impediment, Moses was called into service by the Lord. He would be God's agent to deliver the Hebrews from their oppressors. He, brother Aaron, and tribal leaders presented themselves to Pharaoh requesting the release of the people to worship Yahweh, their God. Pharaoh refuses repeated pleas; the country is subjected to plagues that devastate the land, its natural resources, and in the end resulted in the death of all its first born, animals and people, before releasing the people.

Leadership Maxims: Learn to look beyond surface traits: age, gender, or infirmities; form opinions of value and worth based on firsthand knowledge. Stubborn refusal to face facts is detrimental, often in the extreme.

ⁱⁱⁱ**Solomon** - Son of king David of Israel, author, musician, businessman, inventor, architect and builder. Last king of a united Israel.

As a young king, perhaps less than twenty years old, Solomon succeeded to the throne of a unified Israel secured by his father king David. His forty-year reign brought the nation into its zenith of splendor, wealth, and renown..

From his youth, Solomon was schooled and nurtured in the Hebrew faith, received the best education, and was trained to be a king. Throughout the known world Solomon's reputation was unrivaled and remains legendary.

Gifted with extraordinary wisdom, exceptional creative genius, blessed with enormous wealth, and a remarkable vision for the nation, he brought about an unprecedented period of prosperity and a forty-year peace that has since never been replicated. Israeli commerce flourished. Silver was made as common as stones. Great displays of wealth throughout the city made it a destination point for travelers far and wide. When reading people and issuing judgments he was skilled with an uncanny sense of knowing the truth of a situation.

Yet in the waning days of his life, he abandoned the teachings of youth, the warnings of his parents, and in practice rejected his God. It's nearly inconceivable that the man to whom the Lord appeared twice, spoke with directly, and was so greatly gifted by his Maker would also be the hand that set-in motion the eventual destruction of all that had been his life's pursuits.

After his death, in the reign of his son Rehoboam, the united kingdom of Israel divided north from south leading to invasion, the riches of the city and temple treasure repeatedly plundered, and ultimately the complete destruction of both ended with the forced dispersion and subjugation of the people.

Leadership Maxim: Birth right, lineage, privilege, talent, and fame mean nothing; first from the gate does not guarantee victory. Staying the course is the goal.

[iv]**Queen Esther**- Jewess descendant of Kish, a Benjamite carried captive into Persia in the reign of Nebuchadnezzar. Early orphaned, raised by a first cousin Mordecai as his daughter. Queen of Persia, wife to king Ahasuerus (Xerxes I).

Infuriated by queen Vashti's refusal to appear at court in response to a royal summons Ahasuerus banished her. Esther is chosen from among beauty pageant contestants as the new queen. With the passage of time Esther enjoyed exalted status and was often greeted and recognized by her husband, the king.

Haman, another of the king's favorites, became obsessed with the annihilation of all the Jews, and Mordecai in particular. Owing to his insider status and proximity to the king Haman was able to convince him, along with a great sum of money paid to the treasury, that the Hebrews were in violation of kingdom laws and worthy only of death. So sure was he about the success of his plot, Haman had a huge gallows built and there intended to hang the hated and despised Mordecai. But Haman did not know that Esther was a Jew.

As his extermination plot became known chaos struck the city. The Jews went into deep mourning, fasting and donning sackcloth covered with ashes- the Jewish symbol of bereavement. Mordecai followed the street as far as the king's gate risking immediate punishment for wearing sackcloth was outlawed in the king's court.

Esther quickly intervenes and through a series of exchanged messages Mordecai persuades her to speak with the king on behalf of her people. After a three day fast, Esther stood in the king's inner court and again he acknowledged her asking, [3]... *"What do you wish, Queen Esther? ...* [4]*So Esther answered, "If it pleases the king, let the king and Haman come today to the banquet that I have prepared for him."*

During the festivities the king continued to press Esther for her petition. Bravely she spoke, naming Haman as the enemy. Greatly angered, the king stepped away into a nearby palace garden, but the queen remained reclining on her couch. Falling to his knees before her, Haman begged for his life throwing himself onto her couch. At that precise moment, the king returned, saw Haman sprawled across the queen and concluded he was attempting to assault her. He is sentenced to death– hung on the very gallows intended for Mordecai.

Leadership Maxims: It often happens that the one weaving an evil plot suffers themselves the end devised for another. The selfish, weak-minded, and greedy are drawn-in and persuaded by offers of personal gain. You don't know what you don't know; be alert, cultivate sharp listening and discernment skills.

^v**Deborah-** Hebrew prophetess, leader, and judge in Israel; loved and revered by the people, faithful to rabbinic practice. Deborah lived under her palm tree impartially dispensing the Lord's justice in Israel for 60 years.

Occupation of Canaanite land had grown stagnate. Deborah summoned Barak, general of Hebrew forces, and chided his inaction urging and ordering him forward at the Lord's command. Hebrew forces prevailed, the Jews gained their promised land, and thereafter lived in a period of peace for 40 years.

Leadership Maxims: Gender is no determinant in the skill to lead; people will follow and believe in those demonstrating strength of purpose and commitment to right action. Living a simple unassuming life tends to keep pride and ego at bay in the powerful.

[vi]**George Washington-** Planter, Inventor, Commanding General of American forces in the Revolution, 1st American President.

Washington is one of the most revered and well-remembered men in American history. During his tenure as Commander of American forces in the Revolution he endured bitter rivalries, betrayals, and intense jealousies among his General Staff. Fearing disloyalty from subordinates he often kept his own counsel. Arnold, one of his most trusted field commanders actually turned traitor to the American cause.

Only those who have walked the path can imagine the heavy weight of responsibility and sadness that he shouldered in silence waiting for the right time to expose the treachery that surrounded him so as not to damage the American cause. As President his cabinet members held rancorous animosities toward each other. Meetings often erupted into bitter feuds.

At the end of his second term Washington stepped back from the seat of power when he could easily have become a ruler for life. Rather, he chose retirement from public life and work on the family estate, Mount Vernon.

Leadership Maxims: Waiting for the right time is a discipline that must be cultivated. Betrayal is a given, putting full faith in others is always a risk; be willing to trust but verify. Stepping from the limelight into the shadow is the evidence of self-worth and confidence that is not seized with jealousy toward up-and-coming colleagues.

[vii]**William Wilberforce-** Parliamentarian, humanitarian, devout Christian.

Wilberforce led Britians in the movement to first abolish the slave trade, and later the abolition of slavery itself in the British empire. The work took decades, consumed his life, and wreaked havoc on his health.

Leadership Maxims: When you believe in, and are propelled by a just cause missing the mark is viewed as an opportunity to change course. We learn more effectively through failure when its lessons are remembered, critically evaluated, and put into the proper perspective.

[viii]**Abraham Lincoln**- Lawyer, American Statesman, 16th President of the United States. Commander in Chief of Federal Forces during the American Civil War, eradicated chattel slavery in America.

Lincoln, arguably the most revered man in American history, was propelled by deeply held convictions of human worth. His impoverished youth combined with his reading of the Declaration of Independence occasioned a commitment to upholding human dignity that altered the course of American history and ultimately took his life.

His father, a man less impressed with learning and knowledge than was his son, exerted an oppressive control that gave young Lincoln firsthand experience with exploitation and the yearning to break free from oppressive bonds.

His mother taught him to read, a skill that lighted an eternal flame. His romance with reading stimulated the desire for a life beyond the poverty of his youth and nurtured a gift in language that gave profound expression to ideas of equality. His writing drew heavily from scripture unleashing powerfully framed argument with enormous impact bringing into sharp relief the status quo of the times.

Throughout his adult life Lincoln suffered bouts of melancholia that coincided with low periods when goals seemed unattainable. As President his cabinet members felt themselves infinitely superior in appearance, knowledge, deportment, talent, and vision. But in the end, to a man, his affability, diplomacy, cordiality, intellect, and sense of humor won them over.

Leadership Maxims: Cause is the catalyst that drives change. Graciousness toward those believing themselves superior is humility in action. Masterful use of language is the tool that gives voice to the thoughts, emotions, and experience of others.

Think on this...
We are doomed to repeat what we refuse to right from history. Resolve to study and appropriate the lessons left by those preceding us. Analyze personality traits, events and outcomes; examine motives, causes, objectives, and methods.

In the principled leader, understand that no one is perfect; expecting faultlessness is unrealistic. In the unprincipled leader, determine not to embrace the same driving motives or emulate their actions.

Servant leaders experience the same highs and lows of life that are common to everyone. The marked difference- they persevere through the lows and use the lessons learned to build positive highs.

Feeding the Spirit

It is absurd for a culture that rejects and destroys the notion of accountability to God to expect righteous behavior from its masses. Separation from the source that defines righteousness leaves no base from which to claim the expectation.

[3]if the foundations are destroyed, what can the righteous do? Psalm 11 [ESV]

General perceptions are that character matters not but know this- it is the foundation of personal conviction and conduct. Those in positions of authority that repeatedly demonstrate a lack of character are rudderless and unprincipled. How then can they be trusted with matters of another's wellbeing?

Wisdom is for the Wise

The wisdom paradox: only the wise benefit from wisdom.

Leadership Maxims

Wisdom is the right application of understanding, insight, prudence, justice, discretion, discernment, and sound judgment. Qualities demonstrated in conduct.

Do not confuse wisdom with education. Wisdom is the arbiter of all other knowledge while education is formal instruction.

The wise lead by example because of its effectiveness. The ability to influence and inspire others is best served by example.

The wise understand:
- when "no" is an acceptable solution, when failure has progressed far enough.
- the distinction between managing assets and leading people.
- building effective teams that are solution oriented is the goal.
- valuing people is more than lip service. Actions are personal to those affected by them.
- conduct that adheres to upright, trustable standards produces confidence that inspires others to unleash their highest potential.
- their vulnerability when occupying seats of authority and power.

Proverbs 2

[1]My son, if you receive my words, And treasure my commands within you, [2]So that you incline your ear to wisdom, [And] apply your heart to understanding; [3]Yes, if you cry out for discernment, [And] lift up your voice for understanding, [4]If you seek her as silver, And search for her as [for] hidden treasures; [5]Then you will understand the fear of the LORD, And find the knowledge of God.

[6]For the LORD gives wisdom; From His mouth [come] knowledge and understanding; [7]He stores up sound wisdom for the upright; [He is] a shield to those who walk uprightly; [8]He guards the paths of justice, And preserves the way of His saints. [9]Then you will understand righteousness and justice, Equity [and] every good path.

[10]When wisdom enters your heart, And knowledge is pleasant to your soul, [11]Discretion will preserve you; Understanding will keep you, [12]To deliver you from the way of evil, From the man who speaks perverse things, [13]From those who leave the paths of uprightness To walk in the ways of darkness; [14]Who rejoice in doing evil, [And] delight in the perversity of the wicked; [15]Whose ways [are] crooked, And [who are] devious in their paths; [16]To deliver you from the immoral woman, From the seductress [who] flatters with her words, [17]Who forsakes the companion of her youth, And forgets the covenant of her God. [18]For her house leads down to death, And her paths to the dead; [19]None who go to her return, Nor do they regain the paths of life—[20]So you may walk in the way of goodness, And keep [to] the paths of righteousness. [21]For the upright will dwell in the land, And the blameless will remain in it; [22]But the wicked will be cut off from the earth, And the unfaithful will be uprooted from it.

Proverbs 9

[1]Wisdom has built her house, She has hewn out her seven pillars;[2]She has slaughtered her meat, She has mixed her wine, She has also furnished her table. [3]She has sent out her maidens, She cries out from the highest places of the city, [4]"Whoever [is] simple, let him turn in here!" [As for] him who lacks understanding, she says to him,[5]"Come, eat of my bread And drink of the wine I have mixed. [6]Forsake foolishness and live, And go in the way of understanding.

[7]He who corrects a scoffer gets shame for himself, And he who rebukes a wicked [man only] harms himself. [8]Do not correct a scoffer, lest he hate you; Rebuke a wise [man], and he will love you. [9]Give [instruction] to a wise [man], and he will be still wiser; Teach a just [man], and he will increase in learning.

[10]"The fear of the LORD [is] the beginning of wisdom, And the knowledge of the Holy One [is] understanding. [11]For by me your days will be multiplied, And years of life will be added to you. [12]If you are wise, you are wise for yourself, And [if] you scoff, you will bear [it] alone.

[13]A foolish woman is clamorous; [She is] simple, and knows nothing. [14]For she sits at the door of her house, On a seat [by] the highest places of the city,[15]To call to those who pass by, Who go straight on their way:[16]"Whoever [is] simple, let him turn in here"; And [as for] him who lacks understanding, she says to him,[17]"Stolen water is sweet, And bread [eaten] in secret is pleasant." [18]But he does not know that the dead [are] there, [That] her guests [are] in the depths of hell.

Feeding the Spirit

"Get wisdom.." counsels Solomon, because by it all other choices are made.

The Lord is the source of true wisdom, scripture is the storehouse of knowledge that shapes core values. Determine to set your heart (Biblical euphemism for the mind, the soul, the personality, the conscience and understanding) toward the LORD with unwavering confidence that as you desire and seek to understand His knowledge will be opened to you

[5]If any of you lacks wisdom, let him ask of God, who gives to all liberally and without reproach, and it will be given to him. Let him ask in faith, without doubting for he who doubts is like a wave of the sea driven and tossed by the wind. James 1

[13]Who [is] wise and understanding among you? Let him show by good conduct [that] his works [are done] in the meekness of wisdom. [14]But if you have bitter envy and self-seeking in your hearts, do not boast and lie against the truth. [15]This wisdom does not descend from above, but [is] earthly, sensual, demonic. [16]For where envy and self-seeking [exist], confusion and every evil thing [are] there. [17]But the wisdom that is from above is first pure, then peaceable, gentle, willing to yield, full of mercy and good fruits, without partiality and without hypocrisy. [18]Now the fruit of righteousness is sown in peace by those who make peace. James 3

The Heart

Biblical euphemism for the mind, the soul, the personality, knowledge, understanding, and conscience; the seat of all human attributes. In medieval times the strongest part of a castle was its keep. Likewise, the heart is our keep.

Leadership Maxims

Trust the counsel of those that demonstrate they are guided by and committed to truth; they are reliable by nature. Keep confidence with a laudable, knowledgeable mentor that will remind you – you are accountable.

Example principled behavior. Hypocrisy flashes like a neon-sign; walk must match talk otherwise credibility is lost; when in error, acknowledge it.

Guard against character traits that mark you as self-centered, quick tempered, uncaring for the thoughts and emotions of others. Distance yourself from those that show themselves captive to such behaviors.

Extreme or threating circumstances can drive conduct that is later regrettable. Everyone has the capacity to act thoughtlessly, or in haste. Be circumspect, look inward, scrutinize your motives. It's easy to justify wrongful actions when dislike, revenge, anger, or fright-filled emotions rule.

Do not let yourself be persuaded by that which you know is wrong or hurtful to others. Duplicity, at first, can seem so warranted there is no clash with conscience. Discernment lets you see beyond the superficial or the appearance of a situation.

"What goes around comes around." Although it may take years, the harm you inflict on others is paid back exponentially, so have a care if you are prone to damaging others.

Proverbs 3

[1]My son, do not forget my law, But let your heart keep my commands; [2]For length of days and long life And peace they will add to you.

[3]Let not mercy and truth forsake you; Bind them around your neck, Write them on the tablet of your heart,[4][And] so find favor and high esteem In the sight of God and man.

[5]Trust in the LORD with all your heart, And lean not on your own understanding; [6]In all your ways acknowledge Him, And He shall direct your paths.

[7]Do not be wise in your own eyes; Fear the LORD and depart from evil. [8]It will be health to your flesh, And strength to your bones.

[9]Honor the LORD with your possessions, And with the firstfruits of all your increase;[10]So your barns will be filled with plenty, And your vats will overflow with new wine.

[11]My son, do not despise the chastening of the LORD, Nor detest His correction; [12]For whom the LORD loves He corrects, Just as a father the son [in whom] he delights.

[13]Happy [is] the man [who] finds wisdom, And the man [who] gains understanding; [14]For her proceeds [are] better than the profits of silver, And her gain than fine gold. [15]She [is] more precious than rubies, And all the things you may desire cannot compare with her. [16]Length of days [is] in her right hand, In her left hand riches and honor. [17]Her ways [are] ways of pleasantness, And all her paths [are] peace. [18]She [is] a tree of life to those who take hold of her, And happy [are all] who retain her.

[19]The LORD by wisdom founded the earth; By understanding He established the heavens; [20]By His knowledge the depths were broken up, And clouds drop down the dew.

²¹My son, let them not depart from your eyes--Keep sound wisdom and discretion; ²²So they will be life to your soul And grace to your neck. ²³Then you will walk safely in your way, And your foot will not stumble. ²⁴When you lie down, you will not be afraid; Yes, you will lie down and your sleep will be sweet.

²⁵Do not be afraid of sudden terror, Nor of trouble from the wicked when it comes; ²⁶For the LORD will be your confidence, And will keep your foot from being caught.

²⁷*Do not withhold good from those to whom it is due, When it is in the power of your hand to do [so].* ²⁸Do not say to your neighbor, "Go, and come back, And tomorrow I will give [it]," When you have it with you.

²⁹Do not devise evil against your neighbor, For he dwells by you for safety's sake.

³⁰Do not strive with a man without cause, If he has done you no harm.

³¹Do not envy the oppressor, And choose none of his ways; ³²For the perverse [person is] an abomination to the LORD, But His secret counsel [is] with the upright.

³³The curse of the LORD [is] on the house of the wicked, But He blesses the home of the just. ³⁴Surely He scorns the scornful, But gives grace to the humble.

³⁵The wise shall inherit glory, But shame shall be the legacy of fools.

Proverbs 4

¹Hear, [my] children, the instruction of a father, And give attention to know understanding; ²For I give you good doctrine: Do not forsake my law.

³When I was my father's son, Tender and the only one in the sight of my mother, ⁴He also taught me, and said to me: "Let your heart retain my words; Keep my commands, and live. ⁵Get wisdom! Get understanding! Do not forget, nor turn away from the words of my mouth. Do not forsake her, and she will preserve you; Love her, and she will keep you.

⁷Wisdom [is] the principal thing; [Therefore] get wisdom. And in all your getting, get understanding. ⁸Exalt her, and she will promote you; She will bring you honor, when you embrace her. ⁹She will place on your head an ornament of grace; A crown of glory she will deliver to you."

¹⁰Hear, my son, and receive my sayings, And the years of your life will be many. ¹¹I have taught you in the way of wisdom; I have led you in right paths. ¹²When you walk, your steps will not be hindered, And when you run, you will not stumble. ¹³Take firm hold of instruction, do not let go; Keep her, for she [is] your life.

¹⁴Do not enter the path of the wicked, And do not walk in the way of evil. ¹⁵Avoid it, do not travel on it; Turn away from it and pass on. ¹⁶For they do not sleep unless they have done evil; And their sleep is taken away unless they make [someone] fall. ¹⁷For they eat the bread of wickedness, And drink the wine of violence.

¹⁸But the path of the just [is] like the shining sun, That shines ever brighter unto the perfect day.

¹⁹The way of the wicked [is] like darkness; They do not know what makes them stumble.

²⁰My son, give attention to my words; Incline your ear to my sayings. ²¹Do not let them depart from your eyes; Keep them in the midst of your heart; ²²For they [are] life to those who find them, And health to all their flesh.

[23]Keep your heart with all diligence, For out of it [spring] the issues of life. [24]Put away from you a deceitful mouth, And put perverse lips far from you.[25]Let your eyes look straight ahead, And your eyelids look right before you. [26]Ponder the path of your feet, And let all your ways be established. [27]Do not turn to the right or the left; Remove your foot from evil.

Feeding the Spirit[ix]

Study, memorize the Word, it will come to you in times of confusion and adversity when choices are the most difficult. [15]Study to shew thyself approved unto God, a workman that needeth not to be ashamed, rightly dividing the word of truth. II Timothy 2 [KJV]

Righteousness cannot be feigned; Godly conviction from the heart is powerful. There is no substitute for inward peace, the confidence of doing right tends to calm inner turmoil in troubled times. Being settled in mind causes us to be at peace with others, even those that bitterly oppose all we value. *[7]When a man's ways please the LORD, he makes even his enemies to be at peace with him. Proverbs 16 [ESV]*

Human understanding is subject to perversion by worldly influences and norms. Wickedness at first arouses an unsettled feeling but with repetition so hardens the heart (conscience) it no longer disturbs. Guard your heart with all diligence, *[19]For out of the heart proceed evil thoughts, murders, adulteries, fornications, thefts, false witness, blasphemies. Matthew 15*

Openly and honestly bring your concerns, doubts, and fears to the Lord. Pray for wisdom, ask for understanding and discernment. *[5]If any of you lacks wisdom, let him ask of God, who gives to all liberally and without reproach, and it will be given to him. [6]But let him ask in faith, with no doubting, for he who doubts is like a wave of the sea driven and tossed by the wind. James I*

Kinship with the Lord and knowledge of His Word opens dimensions of thought and conduct that the carnal mind cannot understand or appreciate. Weigh conventional thinking carefully. The closer you are bound to the Word the less worldly opinions will influence your decisions.

Life experiences can harden the heart especially in those that feel used or abused. Dwelling continually on past hurts and inflicted wrongs can warp perception and yield a temperament of mind that separates from sound reasoning corrupting the spirit.

[20]And he [Jesus] said, "What comes out of a person is what defiles him. [21]For from within, out of the heart of man, come evil thoughts, sexual immorality, theft, murder, adultery, [22]coveting, wickedness, deceit, sensuality, envy, slander, pride, foolishness. [23]All these evil things come from within, and they defile a person." Mark 7 [ESV]

We live in an era that differs from former times, "right is now called wrong" and "wrong is now called right." Stand fast for that which is right, use the Word as your guide; as you face trials trust in the Lord. Be reminded, Our LORD uses every situation to school and hone behavior. He controls every outcome and will impart the discernment needed to navigate every situation.

[1]Blessed [is] the man who walks not in the counsel of the ungodly, nor stands in the path of sinners, nor sits in the seat of the scornful ;[2]but his delight [is] in the law of the LORD, and in His law he meditates day and night. Psalms 1

Truth & Trust

Truth is the base alloy of trust; personal integrity, sincerity, and judicious use of power engender trust. Cultivate these traits in yourself, example them, and value them in others.

Leadership Maxims

Where there is no commitment to truth any lie, deception, or deceitful practice can be considered acceptable.

The temptation to abuse another or use a situation to personal benefit can suppress right judgement when you have the power to manipulate circumstances.

Using or abusing others to advance in rank or gain an advantage are character defining qualities. When you choose less than upright methods your actions will eventually rebound. Do no harm.

Don't grind, gripe, or gossip; shoulder harshness and protect the powerless in your charge. Be known for your empathy, listening skills, and discernment.

Don't assume all you hear is always right, speak directly with those that have been charged or slandered, measure the truthfulness of what you are told. Know your people.

Everything is personal, to someone, on some level. Using the "this is business" line is scapegoating.

Distancing yourself from how and where the work is accomplished weakens decision making.

Swaying first in one direction then another, based on prevailing opinions demonstrates a lack of conviction and character. Say nothing rather than out yourself as a sycophant that bends with wind.

Proverbs 13

¹A wise son [heeds] his father's instruction, But a scoffer does not listen to rebuke. ²A man shall eat well by the fruit of [his] mouth, But the soul of the unfaithful feeds on violence. ³He who guards his mouth preserves his life, [But] he who opens wide his lips shall have destruction.

⁴The soul of a lazy [man] desires, and [has] nothing; But the soul of the diligent shall be made rich.

⁵A righteous [man] hates lying, But a wicked [man] is loathsome and comes to shame.
⁶Righteousness guards [him whose] way is blameless, But wickedness overthrows the sinner.
⁷There is one who makes himself rich, yet [has] nothing; [And] one who makes himself poor, yet [has] great riches.
⁸The ransom of a man's life [is] his riches, But the poor does not hear rebuke.
⁹The light of the righteous rejoices, But the lamp of the wicked will be put out.
¹⁰By pride comes nothing but strife, But with the well-advised [is] wisdom.
¹¹Wealth [gained by] dishonesty will be diminished, But he who gathers by labor will increase.
¹²Hope deferred makes the heart sick, But [when] the desire comes, [it is] a tree of life.
¹³He who despises the word will be destroyed, But he who fears the commandment will be rewarded.
¹⁴The law of the wise [is] a fountain of life, To turn [one] away from the snares of death.
¹⁵Good understanding gains favor, But the way of the unfaithful [is] hard.
¹⁶Every prudent [man] acts with knowledge, But a fool lays open [his] folly.
¹⁷A wicked messenger falls into trouble, But a faithful ambassador [brings] health.
¹⁸Poverty and shame [will come] to him who disdains correction, But he who regards a rebuke will be honored.

¹⁹A desire accomplished is sweet to the soul, But [it is] an abomination to fools to depart from evil.

²⁰He who walks with wise [men] will be wise, But the companion of fools will be destroyed.

²¹Evil pursues sinners, But to the righteous, good shall be repaid.

²²A good [man] leaves an inheritance to his children's children, But the wealth of the sinner is stored up for the righteous.

²³Much food [is in] the fallow [ground] of the poor, And for lack of justice there is waste.

²⁴He who spares his rod hates his son, But he who loves him disciplines him promptly.

²⁵The righteous eats to the satisfying of his soul, But the stomach of the wicked shall be in want.

Proverbs 16

¹The preparations of the heart [belong] to man, But the answer of the tongue [is] from the LORD. ²All the ways of a man [are] pure in his own eyes, But the LORD weighs the spirits. ³Commit your works to the LORD, And your thoughts will be established.

⁴The LORD has made all for Himself, Yes, even the wicked for the day of doom.

⁵Everyone proud in heart [is] an abomination to the LORD; [Though they join] forces, none will go unpunished.

⁶In mercy and truth atonement is provided for iniquity; And by the fear of the LORD [one] departs from evil.

⁷When a man's ways please the LORD, He makes even his enemies to be at peace with him.

⁸Better [is] a little with righteousness, Than vast revenues without justice.

⁹A man's heart plans his way, But the LORD directs his steps.

¹⁰Divination [is] on the lips of the king; His mouth must not transgress in judgment.

¹¹Honest weights and scales [are] the LORD's; All the weights in the bag [are] His work.

¹²[It is] an abomination for kings to commit wickedness, For a throne is established by righteousness.

¹³Righteous lips [are] the delight of kings, And they love him who speaks [what is] right.

¹⁴As messengers of death [is] the king's wrath, But a wise man will appease it.

¹⁵In the light of the king's face [is] life, And his favor [is] like a cloud of the latter rain.

¹⁶How much better to get wisdom than gold! And to get understanding is to be chosen rather than silver.

¹⁷The highway of the upright [is] to depart from evil; He who keeps his way preserves his soul.

¹⁸Pride [goes] before destruction, And a haughty spirit before a fall.

¹⁹Better [to be] of a humble spirit with the lowly, Than to divide the spoil with the proud.

²⁰He who heeds the word wisely will find good, And whoever trusts in the LORD, happy [is] he.

²¹The wise in heart will be called prudent, And sweetness of the lips increases learning.

²²Understanding [is] a wellspring of life to him who has it. But the correction of fools [is] folly.

²³The heart of the wise teaches his mouth, And adds learning to his lips.

²⁴Pleasant words [are like] a honeycomb, Sweetness to the soul and health to the bones.

²⁵There is a way [that seems] right to a man, But its end [is] the way of death.

²⁶The person who labors, labors for himself, For his [hungry] mouth drives him [on].

²⁷An ungodly man digs up evil, And [it is] on his lips like a burning fire.

²⁸A perverse man sows strife, And a whisperer separates the best of friends.

²⁹A violent man entices his neighbor, And leads him in a way [that is] not good.³⁰He winks his eye to devise perverse things; He purses his lips [and] brings about evil.

³¹The silver-haired head [is] a crown of glory, [If] it is found in the way of righteousness.

³²[He who is] slow to anger [is] better than the mighty, And he who rules his spirit than he who takes a city.

³³The lot is cast into the lap, But its every decision [is] from the LORD.

Feeding the Spirit

You cannot trust that which you do not rightly know. Study and know the Word, this is only line of defense between the real and the counterfeit.

For the Christian, truth is not relegated to factual utterance only; it embodies the reliability of scripture, reliance on the Word as the definition of man's responsibility to God as his Creator and Savior. When we believe the truthfulness of scripture, we are able to trust in our Lord as our safeguard and deliverer. *6Jesus said to him, "I am the way, the truth, and the life. John 14*

1[A Psalm] of David. To You, O LORD, I lift up my soul. 2O my God, I trust in You; Let me not be ashamed; Let not my enemies triumph over me. 3Indeed, let no one who waits on You be ashamed; Let those be ashamed who deal treacherously without cause.
4Show me Your ways, O LORD; Teach me Your paths. 5Lead me in Your truth and teach me, For You [are] the God of my salvation; On You I wait all the day. Psalm 25

7In God [is] my salvation and my glory; The rock of my strength, [And] my refuge, [is] in God. 8Trust in Him at all times, you people; Pour out your heart before Him; God [is] a refuge for us. Selah Psalm 62

The Bucket of the Mouth

"What is in the well of the heart comes up through the bucket of the mouth."
A Wise Old Sage

Leadership Maxims

Mastering effective communication is just as important as developing strategy. Knowledge and experience are of little value when the inability to effectively communicate is widespread.

Peppering communications with leadership platitudes while the aggregate flounders, is to "fiddle while Rome burns." Letting yourself believe that broadcasting the words of other greats will inspire the masses minus positive action outs you as a do nothing.

Learn to mean what you say, be in possession of all the facts. Never yell, it betrays a loss of self-control, and never let the prevailing wind be your decision-making criteria.

Effective use of language takes perseverance, discipline, knowledge, and practice. Use hyper-descriptive power language to strengthen a point. Reading, listening, and vocabulary building are the best methods to enhance communication skills.

Repeated use of superfluous words, e.g. *like and awesome*, is a distraction that weakens the message. Likewise, slang, i.e. *sweet, sick, cheugy, fleek* has generational significance only; slang originated in the 1960's means nothing to us today.

Cursing laced speech betrays the lack of personal standards of conduct, self-control, and professionalism. Don't let it be part of your speech and never address a subordinate using swearwords.

Listen twice as much as you speak. Often saying nothing is best; you needn't reveal your every thought the moment you have it. Sensing the right moment to speak is critical to making and sticking the point.

Regulate your thoughts in times of extreme stress, chaos, and crisis. Ignore personal insults, focus on events and circumstances to reinforce a point. Chaotic times can present a reason to act in a proposed prescriptive manner.

When total agreement without discussion or challenge is routine, autocracy rules. Check yourself, shutting down discussion that differs from your own opinion limits the extent of the possible and results in courses of action that are one person deep.

Intents and aims are unmasked during conversation. Draw others out; unfettered discussion tends to expose concealed character traits and yearnings.

Short, intemperate responses betray irritation, a lack of self-control, and communicate ridicule or blame. Monitor conversation so as not to stir-up anger or resentment in others. Word wounds have long memories; once said, a thing cannot be un-said.

We are conditioned to think all is made right with a simple apology. Apologize and all is put away and forgotten, but once inflicted wrongful deeds have long memories. Human emotions, wounds, and feelings run deep. Steer clear of actions that damage and cause others pain.

There is always that person that must speak and persistently reveals a lack of knowledge, understanding nothing; DON'T LET IT BE YOU! When you choose to speak be in control, have the facts, understand the circumstances and your audience, keep on point and don't let yourself be drawn down the rabbit hole!

Proverbs 15

¹A soft answer turns away wrath, But a harsh word stirs up anger. ²The tongue of the wise uses knowledge rightly, But the mouth of fools pours forth foolishness.

³The eyes of the LORD [are] in every place, Keeping watch on the evil and the good.

⁴A wholesome tongue [is] a tree of life, But perverseness in it breaks the spirit.
⁵A fool despises his father's instruction, But he who receives correction is prudent.

⁶[In] the house of the righteous [there is] much treasure, But in the revenue of the wicked is trouble.
⁷The lips of the wise disperse knowledge, But the heart of the fool [does] not [do] so.
⁸The sacrifice of the wicked [is] an abomination to the LORD, But the prayer of the upright [is] His delight.
⁹The way of the wicked [is] an abomination to the LORD, But He loves him who follows righteousness.
¹⁰Harsh discipline [is] for him who forsakes the way, [And] he who hates correction will die.
¹¹Hell and Destruction [are] before the LORD; So how much more the hearts of the sons of men.
¹²A scoffer does not love one who corrects him, Nor will he go to the wise.

¹³A merry heart makes a cheerful countenance, But by sorrow of the heart the spirit is broken.
¹⁴The heart of him who has understanding seeks knowledge, But the mouth of fools feeds on foolishness.
¹⁵All the days of the afflicted [are] evil, But he who is of a merry heart [has] a continual feast. ¹⁶Better [is] a little with the fear of the LORD, Than great treasure with trouble. ¹⁷Better [is] a dinner of herbs where love is, Than a fatted calf with hatred.

¹⁸A wrathful man stirs up strife, But [he who is] slow to anger allays contention.

¹⁹The way of the lazy [man is] like a hedge of thorns, But the way of the upright [is] a highway.

²⁰A wise son makes a father glad, But a foolish man despises his mother.

²¹Folly [is] joy [to him who is] destitute of discernment, But a man of understanding walks uprightly.

²²Without counsel, plans go awry, But in the multitude of counselors they are established.

²³A man has joy by the answer of his mouth, And a word [spoken] in due season, how good [it is]!

²⁴The way of life [winds] upward for the wise, That he may turn away from hell below.

²⁵The LORD will destroy the house of the proud, But He will establish the boundary of the widow.

²⁶The thoughts of the wicked [are] an abomination to the LORD, But the words of the pure [are] pleasant.

²⁷He who is greedy for gain troubles his own house, But he who hates bribes will live.

²⁸The heart of the righteous studies how to answer, But the mouth of the wicked pours forth evil.

²⁹The LORD [is] far from the wicked, But He hears the prayer of the righteous.

³⁰The light of the eyes rejoices the heart, [And] a good report makes the bones healthy.

³¹The ear that hears the rebukes of life Will abide among the wise. ³²He who disdains instruction despises his own soul, But he who heeds rebuke gets understanding.

³³The fear of the LORD [is] the instruction of wisdom, And before honor [is] humility.

Proverbs 18

¹A man who isolates himself seeks his own desire; He rages against all wise judgment.
²A fool has no delight in understanding, But in expressing his own heart.
³When the wicked comes, contempt comes also; And with dishonor [comes] reproach.
⁴The words of a man's mouth [are] deep waters; The wellspring of wisdom [is] a flowing brook.

⁵[It is] not good to show partiality to the wicked, [Or] to overthrow the righteous in judgment.
⁶A fool's lips enter into contention, And his mouth calls for blows.
⁷A fool's mouth [is] his destruction, And his lips [are] the snare of his soul.
⁸The words of a talebearer [are] like tasty trifles, And they go down into the inmost body.

⁹He who is slothful in his work Is a brother to him who is a great destroyer.
¹⁰The name of the LORD [is] a strong tower; The righteous run to it and are safe.
¹¹The rich man's wealth [is] his strong city, And like a high wall in his own esteem.
¹²Before destruction the heart of a man is haughty, And before honor [is] humility.

¹³He who answers a matter before he hears [it], It [is] folly and shame to him.

¹⁴The spirit of a man will sustain him in sickness, But who can bear a broken spirit?
¹⁵The heart of the prudent acquires knowledge, And the ear of the wise seeks knowledge.
¹⁶A man's gift makes room for him, And brings him before great men.

[17]The first [one] to plead his cause [seems] right, Until his neighbor comes and examines him.

[18]Casting lots causes contentions to cease, And keeps the mighty apart.

[19]A brother offended [is harder to win] than a strong city, And contentions [are] like the bars of a castle.

[20]A man's stomach shall be satisfied from the fruit of his mouth; [From] the produce of his lips he shall be filled.

[21]Death and life [are] in the power of the tongue, And those who love it will eat its fruit.

[22][He who] finds a wife finds a good [thing], And obtains favor from the LORD.

[23]The poor [man] uses entreaties, But the rich answers roughly.

[24]A man [who has] friends must himself be friendly, But there is a friend [who] sticks closer than a brother.

Feeding the Spirit

Most people are prone to talk too much and interfere in matters not their own. Guard against prying, meddling, and snooping; when trouble arises due to such actions you will be clear of fault. Scripture exhorts us to [11]*study to be quiet and mind your own business... 1 Thessalonian 4 [KJV]*

Take a dim view of swearing and don't let it be part of your speech. [29]No foul language should come from your mouth, but only what is good for building up someone in need, ... Ephesians 4 [CSB]

Strive to keep issues of temper under proper control. [4]Be angry, and do not sin. Meditate within your heart on your bed and be still. Selah Psalm 4

[26]Be angry, and do not sin; do not let the sun go down on your wrath Ephesians 4

Humility vs Pride

Humility is power under control; a proper understanding of humility keeps pride and ego in check.

Leadership Maxims

Pride and ego will always be the biggest self-challenge to face and manage.

Authority, power, and position have an overreaching tendency to inflate ego. Don't think more highly of yourself than is warranted, keeping a right self-image tempers pride.

Singing your own praises reveals a wanton need for attention. Prideful self-exaltation is devoid of fulfillment and never satisfies the need for recognition. When tempted to "toot your own horn" pull back, examine your motive. Braggadocios boasters crave constant recognition and are repellant company.

Understand and master your strengths but recognize also your weaknesses. Train yourself in the habit of critical self-examination, especially after unpleasant or harsh exchanges with others. Compensate for strength deficiencies in the selection of those that surround you.

Overreaching self-confidence and fits of temper that belittle and berate others creates nothing but loathing and when possible, hidden agendas designed with ruinous intent.

School yourself in the art of seeing from another's viewpoint. Demanding absolute adherence to rules and regulations without regard to circumstances outs adaptability deficiencies; be open to alternate approaches.

Self-absorption with status, power, and position are the marks of prideful arrogance. Demands for personal address indicating rank or title is a blatant sign of autocratic rule.

Make yourself available to those in your sphere of control. Be ready to receive every manner of feedback without defense. Consider, as objectively as possible, everything you hear but rule out the superfluous. Often envy and malicious intent are motives. Change what needs changing, leave the rest on the cutting room floor.

Proverbs 11

¹Dishonest scales [are] an abomination to the LORD, But a just weight [is] His delight.

²When pride comes, then comes shame; But with the humble [is] wisdom. ³The integrity of the upright will guide them, But the perversity of the unfaithful will destroy them.

⁴Riches do not profit in the day of wrath, But righteousness delivers from death.
⁵The righteousness of the blameless will direct his way aright, But the wicked will fall by his own wickedness.
⁶The righteousness of the upright will deliver them, But the unfaithful will be caught by [their] lust.
⁷When a wicked man dies, [his] expectation will perish, And the hope of the unjust perishes.
⁸The righteous is delivered from trouble, And it comes to the wicked instead.

⁹The hypocrite with [his] mouth destroys his neighbor, But through knowledge the righteous will be delivered.
¹⁰When it goes well with the righteous, the city rejoices; And when the wicked perish, [there is] jubilation. ¹¹By the blessing of the upright the city is exalted, But it is overthrown by the mouth of the wicked.
¹²He who is devoid of wisdom despises his neighbor, But a man of understanding holds his peace. ¹³A talebearer reveals secrets, But he who is of a faithful spirit conceals a matter.
¹⁴Where [there is] no counsel, the people fall; But in the multitude of counselors [there is] safety.

¹⁵He who is surety for a stranger will suffer, But one who hates being surety is secure.
¹⁶A gracious woman retains honor, But ruthless [men] retain riches.

¹⁷The merciful man does good for his own soul, But [he who is] cruel troubles his own flesh. ¹⁸The wicked [man] does

deceptive work, But he who sows righteousness [will have] a sure reward.

¹⁹As righteousness [leads] to life, So he who pursues evil [pursues it] to his own death. ²⁰Those who are of a perverse heart [are] an abomination to the LORD, But [the] blameless in their ways [are] His delight. ²¹[Though they join] forces, the wicked will not go unpunished; But the posterity of the righteous will be delivered.

²²[As] a ring of gold in a swine's snout, [So is] a lovely woman who lacks discretion.

²³The desire of the righteous [is] only good, [But] the expectation of the wicked [is] wrath.

²⁴There is [one] who scatters, yet increases more; And there is [one] who withholds more than is right, But it [leads] to poverty. ²⁵The generous soul will be made rich, And he who waters will also be watered himself. ²⁶The people will curse him who withholds grain, But blessing [will be] on the head of him who sells [it].

²⁷He who earnestly seeks good finds favor, But trouble will come to him who seeks [evil].

²⁸He who trusts in his riches will fall, But the righteous will flourish like foliage.

²⁹He who troubles his own house will inherit the wind, And the fool [will be] servant to the wise of heart. ³⁰The fruit of the righteous [is a] tree of life, And he who wins souls [is] wise.

³¹If the righteous will be recompensed on the earth, How much more the ungodly and the sinner.

Proverbs 22

¹Choose a good name rather than great riches, loving favor rather than silver and gold.

²The rich and poor have this in common; the LORD made them both.

³A prudent man sees evil and hides himself but the simpleton keeps going and pays the price.

⁴The reward of humility and the fear of the LORD is wealth, honor, and life.

⁵Thorns and snares are in the way of the perverse, he who guards his soul will be far from them.

⁶Train up a child in the way he should go and when he is old he will not depart from it.

⁷The rich rule over the poor and the borrower is servant to the lender.

⁸Those that spread wickedness shall reap sorrow and the rod of his anger shall fail.

⁹Blessed are the generous because they feed the poor.

¹⁰Drive out the scorner and contention shall cease, yes strife and reproach will stop.

¹¹Those that love purity of heart; the king shall be his friend because of the loveliness of his speech.

¹²The LORD preserves knowledge and He overturns the utterance of transgressor.

¹³The lazy man says: There is a lion abroad, if I go out I shall be killed in the streets.

¹⁴The mouth of an immoral women is a deep pit, he that is abhorred by the LORD shall fall therein.

¹⁵Foolishness is bound in the heart of a child but the rod of correction shall drive it out of him.

¹⁶He that oppresses the poor to increase his riches and he that giveth to the rich shall surely come to want.

¹⁷Incline your ear and hear the words of the wise, apply your heart to my knowledge. ¹⁸For [it is] a pleasant thing if you keep

them in your heart, let them all be fixed upon your lips, [19]so that your trust may be in the LORD; I have instructed you today, even you. [20]Have I not written to you excellent things of counsels and knowledge, [21]that I may make you know the certainty of the words of truth, that you may answer words of truth to those who send to you?

[22]Rob not the poor because he is poor, do not oppress the afflicted in the gate, [23]for the LORD will plead their cause and spoil the soul of those that defraud them.
[24]Make no friendship with an angry man; with a furious man do not go [25]lest you learn his ways and ensnare your own soul.

[26]Be not one of them that shakes hands in a pledge or who secures a debt. [27]When you owe nothing why would someone come and take away your bed from under you?
[28]Do not remove the ancient landmark which your fathers have set.
[29]Do you see a man diligent in his business? He shall stand before kings, not insignificant men.

Proverbs 25

¹These also [are] proverbs of Solomon which the men of Hezekiah king of Judah copied:

²[It is] the glory of God to conceal a matter, But the glory of kings [is] to search out a matter. ³[As] the heavens for height and the earth for depth, So the heart of kings [is] unsearchable.

⁴Take away the dross from silver, And it will go to the silversmith [for] jewelry. ⁵Take away the wicked from before the king, And his throne will be established in righteousness.

⁶Do not exalt yourself in the presence of the king, And do not stand in the place of the great;⁷For [it is] better that he say to you, "Come up here," Than that you should be put lower in the presence of the prince, Whom your eyes have seen.

⁸Do not go hastily to court; For what will you do in the end, When your neighbor has put you to shame?

⁹Debate your case with your neighbor, And do not disclose the secret to another;¹⁰Lest he who hears [it] expose your shame, And your reputation be ruined.

¹¹A word fitly spoken [is like] apples of gold In settings of silver.
¹²[Like] an earring of gold and an ornament of fine gold [Is] a wise rebuker to an obedient ear.

¹³Like the cold of snow in time of harvest [Is] a faithful messenger to those who send him, For he refreshes the soul of his masters.

¹⁴Whoever falsely boasts of giving [Is like] clouds and wind without rain.

¹⁵By long forbearance a ruler is persuaded, And a gentle tongue breaks a bone.

¹⁶Have you found honey? Eat only as much as you need, Lest you be filled with it and vomit.

¹⁷Seldom set foot in your neighbor's house, Lest he become weary of you and hate you.

¹⁸A man who bears false witness against his neighbor [Is like] a club, a sword, and a sharp arrow.
¹⁹Confidence in an unfaithful [man] in time of trouble [Is like] a bad tooth and a foot out of joint.

²⁰[Like] one who takes away a garment in cold weather, [And like] vinegar on soda, [Is] one who sings songs to a heavy heart.
²¹If your enemy is hungry, give him bread to eat; And if he is thirsty, give him water to drink; ²²For [so] you will heap coals of fire on his head, And the LORD will reward you.

²³The north wind brings forth rain, And a backbiting tongue an angry countenance.
²⁴[It is] better to dwell in a corner of a housetop, Than in a house shared with a contentious woman.
²⁵[As] cold water to a weary soul, So [is] good news from a far country.

²⁶A righteous [man] who falters before the wicked [Is like] a murky spring and a polluted well.
²⁷[It is] not good to eat much honey; So to seek one's own glory [is not] glory.
²⁸Whoever [has] no rule over his own spirit [Is like] a city broken down, without walls.

Feeding the Spirit

Pride is at the root of every evil deed; while humility is true piety- a right understanding of the human condition and the sin nature. Haughty, prideful arrogance is destructive, character traits that led Satan to rebellion and will destroy him.

The Lord exerts His control to teach and mold in every situation, even in the face of what appears to be failure. Humility and self-control are often the lessons to learn in adversarial situations.

[13]The fear of the LORD is hatred of evil. Pride and arrogance and the way of evil and perverted speech I hate. Proverbs 8 [ESV]

[18]Pride goes before destruction, and a haughty spirit before a fall. Proverbs 16 [ESV]

[24]"Scoffer" is the name of the arrogant, haughty man who acts with arrogant pride. Proverbs 21 [ESV]

All you achieve is through the good graces of our Lord. He bestows every gift and talent you possess. [3]Do nothing from selfish ambition or conceit, but in humility count others more significant than yourselves. Philippians 2 [ESV]

Knowledge & Discernment

Knowledge, it is said, is power; it is therefore curious that many in power take a narrow view, are so often ill-informed, and exercise so little discernment.

Leadership Maxims

Knowledge is intellectual understanding in accordance with the truth of a matter and separates from opinion by certainty. Discernment is the ability to learn through discrimination, examine and scrutinize circumstances and events.

Knowledge feeds discernment, have command of the facts, and appropriate the information learned.

There is no virtue in intellectual stupidity; use the knowledge gained through education and observation. Intellectual prowess broadens thinking, adds clarity, and helps formulate vision. Rejection of evident truth is foolish; listen and learn.

Knowledge of the past can temper and inform the future. Devaluing or ignoring that which is taught through history is to be ignorant, this applies to personalities and times. What will not be learned and corrected is doomed to repetition.

Doing the same thing and expecting a different result is what Einstein called insanity. Acknowledge errors with course correction that is swift and decisive. Personal observation and wise counsel makes the difference between prudent courses of action and seeing what is ahead rather than repeating failure.

Cultivate the habit of fact checking your opinions. Challenge the specious with facts. Possessing and having command of facts tends to expose feckless, self-serving solutions.

Scrutinize what you hear, measure everything by what is done. Recognize the truth about those in your immediate circle, and yourself. Never take the word of another when forming character opinions, learn firsthand what is true about another.

Ignoring difficult or volatile situations is never a solution. Neglect or inaction is a form of reward that reaps more of the same behavior. Get the facts, seek wise counsel; do what must be done in situations that require strong correction. Explain decisions and the reasons for the actions; do no unnecessary harm.

The unknowing, the self-serving, and sycophantic grovelers are everywhere. Watch, study behavior, weed out when you can, neutralize the rest to back burner activity.

Proverbs 8

[1]Does not wisdom cry out, And understanding lift up her voice? [2]She takes her stand on the top of the high hill, Beside the way, where the paths meet. [3]She cries out by the gates, at the entry of the city, At the entrance of the doors: [4]To you, O men, I call, And my voice [is] to the sons of men.

[5]O you simple ones, understand prudence, And you fools, be of an understanding heart. [6]Listen, for I will speak of things, And from the opening of my lips [will come] right things; [7]For my mouth will speak truth; Wickedness [is] an abomination to my lips. [8]All the words of my mouth [are] with righteousness; Nothing crooked or perverse [is] in them. [9]They [are] all plain to him who understands, And right to those who find knowledge. [10]Receive my instruction, and not silver, And knowledge rather than choice gold;[11]For wisdom [is] better than rubies, And all the things one may desire cannot be compared with her.

[12]"I, wisdom, dwell with prudence, And find out knowledge [and] discretion. [13]The fear of the LORD [is] to hate evil; Pride and arrogance and the evil way And the perverse mouth I hate. [14]Counsel [is] mine, and sound wisdom; I [am] understanding, I have strength. [15]By me kings reign, And rulers decree justice. [16]By me princes rule, and nobles, All the judges of the earth. [17]I love those who love me, And those who seek me diligently will find me.
[18]Riches and honor [are] with me, Enduring riches and righteousness. [19]My fruit [is] better than gold, yes, than fine gold, And my revenue than choice silver. [20]I traverse the way of righteousness, In the midst of the paths of justice, [21]That I may cause those who love me to inherit wealth, That I may fill their treasuries.

[22]"The LORD possessed me at the beginning of His way, Before His works of old. [23]I have been established from everlasting, From the beginning, before there was ever an earth. [24]When [there were] no depths I was brought forth,

When [there were] no fountains abounding with water. ²⁵Before the mountains were settled, Before the hills, I was brought forth; ²⁶While as yet He had not made the earth or the fields, Or the primal dust of the world. ²⁷When He prepared the heavens, I [was] there, When He drew a circle on the face of the deep, ²⁸When He established the clouds above, When He strengthened the fountains of the deep, ²⁹When He assigned to the sea its limit, So that the waters would not transgress His command, When He marked out the foundations of the earth, ³⁰Then I was beside Him [as] a master craftsman; And I was daily [His] delight, Rejoicing always before Him, ³¹Rejoicing in His inhabited world, And my delight [was] with the sons of men.

³²"Now therefore, listen to me, [my] children, For blessed [are those who] keep my ways. ³³Hear instruction and be wise, And do not disdain [it]. ³⁴Blessed is the man who listens to me, Watching daily at my gates, Waiting at the posts of my doors. ³⁵For whoever finds me finds life, And obtains favor from the LORD; ³⁶But he who sins against me wrongs his own soul; All those who hate me love death."

Proverbs 24

¹Do not be envious of evil men, Nor desire to be with them; ²For their heart devises violence, And their lips talk of troublemaking.
³Through wisdom a house is built, And by understanding it is established;⁴By knowledge the rooms are filled With all precious and pleasant riches.

⁵A wise man [is] strong, Yes, a man of knowledge increases strength; ⁶For by wise counsel you will wage your own war, And in a multitude of counselors [there is] safety.
⁷Wisdom [is] too lofty for a fool; He does not open his mouth in the gate. ⁸He who plots to do evil Will be called a schemer. ⁹The devising of foolishness [is] sin, And the scoffer [is] an abomination to men.

¹⁰[If] you faint in the day of adversity, Your strength [is] small.

¹¹Deliver [those who] are drawn toward death, And hold back [those] stumbling to the slaughter. ¹²If you say, "Surely we did not know this," Does not He who weighs the hearts consider [it]? He who keeps your soul, does He [not] know [it]? And will He [not] render to [each] man according to his deeds?

¹³My son, eat honey because [it is] good, And the honeycomb [which is] sweet to your taste;¹⁴So [shall] the knowledge of wisdom [be] to your soul; If you have found [it], there is a prospect, And your hope will not be cut off.

¹⁵Do not lie in wait, O wicked [man], against the dwelling of the righteous; Do not plunder his resting place;¹⁶For a righteous [man] may fall seven times And rise again, But the wicked shall fall by calamity.
¹⁷Do not rejoice when your enemy falls, And do not let your heart be glad when he stumbles;¹⁸Lest the LORD see [it], and it displease Him, And He turn away His wrath from him.

¹⁹Do not fret because of evildoers, Nor be envious of the wicked;²⁰For there will be no prospect for the evil [man]; The lamp of the wicked will be put out.

²¹My son, fear the LORD and the king; Do not associate with those given to change;²²For their calamity will rise suddenly, And who knows the ruin those two can bring?

²³These [things] also [belong] to the wise: [It is] not good to show partiality in judgment.

²⁴He who says to the wicked, "You [are] righteous," Him the people will curse; Nations will abhor him. ²⁵But those who rebuke [the wicked] will have delight, And a good blessing will come upon them. ²⁶He who gives a right answer kisses the lips.

²⁷Prepare your outside work, Make it fit for yourself in the field; And afterward build your house.

²⁸Do not be a witness against your neighbor without cause, For would you deceive with your lips? ²⁹Do not say, "I will do to him just as he has done to me; I will render to the man according to his work."

³⁰I went by the field of the lazy [man], And by the vineyard of the man devoid of understanding;³¹And there it was, all overgrown with thorns; Its surface was covered with nettles; Its stone wall was broken down. ³²When I saw [it], I considered [it] well; I looked on [it and] received instruction: ³³A little sleep, a little slumber, A little folding of the hands to rest;³⁴So shall your poverty come [like] a prowler, And your need like an armed man.

Proverbs 30

¹The words of Agur the son of Jakeh, [his] utterance. This man declared to Ithiel--to Ithiel and Ucal:

²Surely I [am] more stupid than [any] man, And do not have the understanding of a man. ³I neither learned wisdom Nor have knowledge of the Holy One.
⁴Who has ascended into heaven, or descended? Who has gathered the wind in His fists? Who has bound the waters in a garment? Who has established all the ends of the earth? What [is] His name, and what [is] His Son's name, If you know?
⁵Every word of God [is] pure; He [is] a shield to those who put their trust in Him. ⁶Do not add to His words, Lest He rebuke you, and you be found a liar. ⁷Two [things] I request of You (Deprive me not before I die):⁸Remove falsehood and lies far from me; Give me neither poverty nor riches--Feed me with the food allotted to me;⁹Lest I be full and deny [You], And say, "Who [is] the LORD?" Or lest I be poor and steal, And profane the name of my God.

¹⁰Do not malign a servant to his master, Lest he curse you, and you be found guilty.
¹¹[There is] a generation [that] curses its father, And does not bless its mother.
¹²[There is] a generation [that is] pure in its own eyes, [Yet] is not washed from its filthiness.
¹³[There is] a generation--oh, how lofty are their eyes! And their eyelids are lifted up.
¹⁴[There is] a generation whose teeth [are like] swords, And whose fangs [are like] knives, To devour the poor from off the earth, And the needy from [among] men.

¹⁵The leech has two daughters--Give [and] Give! There are three [things that] are never satisfied, Four never say, "Enough!"¹⁶The grave, The barren womb, The earth [that] is not satisfied with water--And the fire never says, "Enough!"

¹⁷The eye [that] mocks [his] father, And scorns obedience to [his] mother, The ravens of the valley will pick it out, And the young eagles will eat it.

¹⁸There are three [things which] are too wonderful for me, Yes, four [which] I do not understand:
¹⁹The way of an eagle in the air, The way of a serpent on a rock, The way of a ship in the midst of the sea, And the way of a man with a virgin.
²⁰This [is] the way of an adulterous woman: She eats and wipes her mouth, And says, "I have done no wickedness."
²¹For three [things] the earth is perturbed, Yes, for four it cannot bear up:²²For a servant when he reigns, A fool when he is filled with food,²³A hateful [woman] when she is married, And a maidservant who succeeds her mistress.
²⁴There are four [things which] are little on the earth, But they [are] exceedingly wise:²⁵The ants [are] a people not strong, Yet they prepare their food in the summer;²⁶The rock badgers are a feeble folk, Yet they make their homes in the crags;²⁷The locusts have no king, Yet they all advance in ranks;²⁸The spider skillfully grasps with its hands, And it is in kings' palaces.
²⁹There are three [things which] are majestic in pace, Yes, four [which] are stately in walk:³⁰A lion, [which is] mighty among beasts And does not turn away from any;³¹A greyhound, A male goat also, And a king [whose] troops [are] with him.

³²If you have been foolish in exalting yourself, Or if you have devised evil, [put your] hand on [your] mouth. ³³For [as] the churning of milk produces butter, And wringing the nose produces blood, So the forcing of wrath produces strife.

Feeding the Spirit

Discipline is a training tool that grows knowledge. Yield to and be instructed by proper discipline.

[2]My brethren, count it all joy when you fall into various trials, [3]knowing that the testing of your faith produces patience. [4]But let patience have [its] perfect work, that you may be perfect and complete, lacking nothing. James 1

In relationships, train yourself to watch behavior; talk is cheap while commitment to right is demonstrated. Make and keep fellowship with those that are honest, principled, and share your values.

It's not all good! Life experiences wound and scar deeply. Experience has the insidious power to shape and channel the future and while some are valuable lessons others can be debilitating and crushing.

The Company We Keep

You will be known by your associations, professionally and personally.

Leadership Maxims

Choose relationships with those that share your values and are evidenced in lifestyle. You will be inspired by and gain confidence from those with whom you have like-mindedness.

Consider your reputation in all you do; liars, cheats, no-loads, and users are abhorred above even the mediocre. Do not stand with or be counted among those that devise or plot harm to others.

Preferential treatment of favorites is noticed and creates deep seated resentment in others.

When you choose unsavory dubious companions, you will be guilty by association. Know this: you are merely one of the horde when you proclaim innocence in the face of misconduct.

Powerful coalitions align to produce end states that service the ambitions of the members.

Controlling membership or having the ability to personally select those in your immediate circle is not always possible– much of the time the hand that is dealt must be played.

Competition for your "ear" will be fierce. As your sphere of authority and power increases, some in your circle will be self-serving and less than truthful.

Quarrelsome, contentious, factious personalities spread nothing but enmity and disruption. Continual states of turmoil or conflict create tension and levels of stress that are untenable in the long term. Be aware of personality-based contention and mere love of strife.

Proverbs 27

¹Do not boast about tomorrow, For you do not know what a day may bring forth.
²Let another man praise you, and not your own mouth; A stranger, and not your own lips.

³A stone [is] heavy and sand [is] weighty, But a fool's wrath [is] heavier than both of them.
⁴Wrath [is] cruel and anger a torrent, But who [is] able to stand before jealousy?
⁵Open rebuke [is] better Than love carefully concealed.
⁶Faithful [are] the wounds of a friend, But the kisses of an enemy [are] deceitful.

⁷A satisfied soul loathes the honeycomb, But to a hungry soul every bitter thing [is] sweet.
⁸Like a bird that wanders from its nest [Is] a man who wanders from his place.

⁹Ointment and perfume delight the heart, And the sweetness of a man's friend [gives delight] by hearty counsel.
¹⁰Do not forsake your own friend or your father's friend, Nor go to your brother's house in the day of your calamity; Better [is] a neighbor nearby than a brother far away.

¹¹My son, be wise, and make my heart glad, That I may answer him who reproaches me.
¹²A prudent [man] foresees evil [and] hides himself; The simple pass on [and] are punished.
¹³Take the garment of him who is surety for a stranger, And hold it in pledge [when] he is surety for a seductress.
¹⁴He who blesses his friend with a loud voice, rising early in the morning, It will be counted a curse to him.
¹⁵A continual dripping on a very rainy day And a contentious woman are alike; ¹⁶Whoever restrains her restrains the wind, And grasps oil with his right hand.

¹⁷[As] iron sharpens iron, So a man sharpens the countenance of his friend.

¹⁸Whoever keeps the fig tree will eat its fruit; So he who waits on his master will be honored.

¹⁹As in water face [reflects] face, So a man's heart [reveals] the man.

²⁰Hell and Destruction are never full; So the eyes of man are never satisfied.

²¹The refining pot [is] for silver and the furnace for gold, And a man [is valued] by what others say of him.

²²Though you grind a fool in a mortar with a pestle along with crushed grain, [Yet] his foolishness will not depart from him.

²³Be diligent to know the state of your flocks, [And] attend to your herds; ²⁴For riches [are] not forever, Nor does a crown [endure] to all generations.

²⁵[When] the hay is removed, and the tender grass shows itself, And the herbs of the mountains are gathered in, ²⁶The lambs [will provide] your clothing, And the goats the price of a field; ²⁷[You shall have] enough goats' milk for your food, For the food of your household, And the nourishment of your maidservants.

Feeding the Spirit

Once gained bad repute follows relentlessly. [1]A good name [is] better than precious ointment, Ecclesiastes 7

The company we keep has effect; evil urges evil deeds, while the upright encourage truth and virtue. When the conscience is bothered, listen to its warning; do not sacrifice peace of mind for friendships or beneficial connections.

Choose relationships with those whose conversation and interests in spiritual matters, personal deportment, and professional conduct raises the bar to higher standards.

Close relationships can become familial in character. Value true friends, those that share your values and strengthen your spirit. Treat them with kindness, charity, and consideration.

It is far more gratifying to receive an invitation rather than pushing your way into a group. [10]But when you are invited, go and sit down in the lowest place, so that when he who invited you comes he may say to you, 'Friend, go up higher.' Then you will have glory in the presence of those who sit at the table with you. Luke 14

Work-Life Balance

Sacrificing family to attain career goals is in the end void of gratification and happiness. Family relationships sustain you; make home the solid foundation from which you operate.

Leadership Maxims

Often our family members form the best circle of accountability when your welfare and wellbeing are their first consideration.

Often family members are keen observers of character, listen to their counsel; they know you best and have courage enough to confront.

Home and work require your attention and both have legitimate claims on your time and concentration. Be focused where you are – when at home be at home, when at work be at work. Master time management skills and focus.

- Schedule activities and plan family outings that stimulate effective communication and create loving bonds of affection. Your spouse must be first in your affection. Plan dates with your spouse; and outings with children that give them your undivided attention. Make it a priority to know their likes, dislikes, and aspirations; step outside your comfort zone to accommodate an interest. Plan vacation time that is a total separation from work to focus on your family; set boundaries that are rigidly enforced. In older children, let them experience you as advisor and counselor; bring alternate perspectives and approaches or thinking that help them see through concerns or emotional stresses. Help them understand that when you are at work you need to be focused to the same degree barring emergencies.

- Work associates and subordinates have a right to expect your commitment to goals and objectives. Demonstrated focus, experience, reliability, and commitment create team bonds and trust. Interrupting critical discussion or decision making meetings with family calls that are not emergency related is disrespectful to associates and communicates an aura of unimportance.

Last thought, substituting phone calls, anytime anywhere, will not compensate for neglected family duties and the lack of parental presence at home.

Military & Government Service
Participation in the military and positions in government service are among the most time demanding jobs. Duties and assignments can call for prolonged periods of separation that disrupt family cohesion. For relationships to work well family members must support the service member's obligations and understand the need to be apart.

In function, the home front must be able to operate in a semi-independent state with surety that decisions will be supported. Mate selection is critical in this capacity, there must be an element of self-reliance and strength of character that can sustain separations, be faithful, and lead the family.

Although a physical presence is the optimum family model in today's high tech environment communication need not be a casualty of separation. When apart, the service member, to the greatest extent possible, should prioritize and keep communication with the family a constant. Scheduling regular times can be helpful to ensure all family members are present and get time and a share of the focus.

Last thought, accepting absenteeism means missing critical interaction that bond family members in ways that exclude the service member. You must be willing to accept the emotional separation it creates and may never be forgotten.

Proverbs 31

¹The words of King Lemuel, the utterance which his mother taught him: ²What, my son? And what, son of my womb? And what, son of my vows?

³Do not give your strength to women, Nor your ways to that which destroys kings. ⁴[It is] not for kings, O Lemuel, [It is] not for kings to drink wine, Nor for princes intoxicating drink; ⁵Lest they drink and forget the law, And pervert the justice of all the afflicted. ⁶Give strong drink to him who is perishing, And wine to those who are bitter of heart. ⁷Let him drink and forget his poverty, And remember his misery no more. ⁸Open your mouth for the speechless, In the cause of all [who are] appointed to die. ⁹Open your mouth, judge righteously, And plead the cause of the poor and needy.

¹⁰Who can find a virtuous wife? For her worth [is] far above rubies.
¹¹The heart of her husband safely trusts her; So he will have no lack of gain.
¹²She does him good and not evil All the days of her life.
¹³She seeks wool and flax, And willingly works with her hands.
¹⁴She is like the merchant ships, She brings her food from afar.
¹⁵She also rises while it is yet night, And provides food for her household, And a portion for her maidservants.
¹⁶She considers a field and buys it; From her profits she plants a vineyard.
¹⁷She girds herself with strength, And strengthens her arms.
¹⁸She perceives that her merchandise [is] good, And her lamp does not go out by night.
¹⁹She stretches out her hands to the distaff, And her hand holds the spindle.
²⁰She extends her hand to the poor, Yes, she reaches out her hands to the needy.
²¹She is not afraid of snow for her household, For all her household [is] clothed with scarlet.
²²She makes tapestry for herself; Her clothing [is] fine linen and purple.

²³Her husband is known in the gates, When he sits among the elders of the land.

²⁴She makes linen garments and sells [them], And supplies sashes for the merchants.

²⁵Strength and honor [are] her clothing; She shall rejoice in time to come.

²⁶She opens her mouth with wisdom, And on her tongue [is] the law of kindness.

²⁷She watches over the ways of her household, And does not eat the bread of idleness.

²⁸Her children rise up and call her blessed; Her husband [also], and he praises her: ²⁹"Many daughters have done well, But you excel them all."

³⁰Charm [is] deceitful and beauty [is] passing, But a woman [who] fears the LORD, she shall be praised.

³¹Give her of the fruit of her hands, And let her own works praise her in the gates.

Feeding the Spirit

The Proverbs 31 model is service to the family. Scripture is a rich source for family studies, all are portrayed as they lived. Be guided by their successes and failures.

Men bear the responsibility before God for the family; leave off petty bickering, strife, harshness, and autocratic rule; be the trustworthy benevolent lover, generous mate, and life partner your spouse deserves; praise her lavishly and openly.

Although womanhood and notions of femininity have changed with the passage of time the strength and impact of wife and mother in the family is one of dignity, marked by intellect, diligent work and service. Be a united front with your spouse in all things, remembering every issue is not one for argument.

Expecting perfection in all things from yourself and others is a certain recipe for bitter disappointment and crushing defeat. We are all imperfect beings; tolerance, kindness, forbearance, and forgiveness are our by words. Knowing does not always translate to action, the larger goal is staying the course-reshaping the mind (thinking) and bringing our actions (the will) under subjection to Godly control is a lifelong pursuit.

Mentoring

Balancing people-needs and mission goals is tough in the best of circumstances but doubles down in the midst of chaos. Finding the middle ground between mission and people is a monumental challenge.

Leadership Maxims

Motivation is seeded and flowers from within. Find something you love, something that gives you purpose and drives you to action. One of the worst things at the end of life is looking back with sour regret on wasted time.

Assume your career aspirations and desires are similar to those within your sphere of control. Strive to provide an environment in which others can thrive and reach maximum potential. The whole benefits from the industry of each member.

People that advance based on quota systems or networked connection are unlikely to step back even when painfully out of depth. Favoritism is quickly "outed" breeding contempt and disrespect in others, especially when known friends are among the favored.

Watch for talent in the available resource pool to groom and advance into future leadership roles. Make this a cultural standard. Strive for impartiality in your choices.

Invest time and effort in others, share your knowledge and expertise; provide helpful suggestions or things to consider where possible. The servant leader maintains a sharp focus on the welfare of those in their charge but know when to say when. Regardless of what you do, some people are never satiated or understand their failings in a prudential light.

Technical prowess does not automatically translate to leadership acumen. In the final analysis knowledge is wasted, and ineffective supervision that does more harm than good is empowered.

Don't inflict damage on effective teams by advancing the immature and unprepared into positions of authority. The most talented and valued resources will abandon the team for other opportunities in the face of poor team leadership.

Diplomacy is a skill, seek and keep those who have it mastered in your inner circle. Learn from and empower them to smooth distressed waters.

A broken spirit is debilitating in ways that can be disabling. Saying, "Don't, or you shouldn't, feel that way." is a shallow, superficial, thoughtless attempt to salve a wound. Thoughts, focus, and experiences program feelings. Encouragement is most meaningful when offered in terms of surrendering the power of self-worth -- giving another the power to shape how you think about yourself. Never give people that care nothing for you the power of controlling your thoughts.

Work reviews can be challenging to affect with positive outcomes. Leaving the impression that work has been substandard is always the risk. If the work is a good start communicate that openly. Leave off word-smithing and unnecessary criticism that adds no value. Peer view is helpful but make it a team standard that applies to everyone.

Advising or offering correction is thorny even in the best of situations and relationships. Earn the right to speak openly. Creating an atmosphere of caring is an essential, wait for circumstances that demonstrate why shifts in thinking is important. When offering counsel, be sure there is no perceived "pay day" that is self-serving.

Stop repeating what you hear as if it's your idea; check yourself with, "This is what I think I heard ..., help me understand if I am wrong."

Refrain from beginning every response with the word NO. This is the mark of a manager, not a leader.

Proverbs 14

¹The wise woman builds her house, But the foolish pulls it down with her hands.

²He who walks in his uprightness fears the LORD, But [he who is] perverse in his ways despises Him. ³In the mouth of a fool [is] a rod of pride, But the lips of the wise will preserve them.

⁴Where no oxen [are], the trough [is] clean; But much increase [comes] by the strength of an ox.

⁵A faithful witness does not lie, But a false witness will utter lies.
⁶A scoffer seeks wisdom and does not [find it], But knowledge [is] easy to him who understands.
⁷Go from the presence of a foolish man, When you do not perceive [in him] the lips of knowledge. ⁸The wisdom of the prudent [is] to understand his way, But the folly of fools [is] deceit. ⁹Fools mock at sin, But among the upright [there is] favor.

¹⁰The heart knows its own bitterness, And a stranger does not share its joy.
¹¹The house of the wicked will be overthrown, But the tent of the upright will flourish.
¹²There is a way [that seems] right to a man, But its end [is] the way of death.
¹³Even in laughter the heart may sorrow, And the end of mirth [may be] grief.
¹⁴The backslider in heart will be filled with his own ways, But a good man [will be satisfied] from above.

¹⁵The simple believes every word, But the prudent considers well his steps.
¹⁶A wise [man] fears and departs from evil, But a fool rages and is self-confident.
¹⁷A quick-tempered [man] acts foolishly, And a man of wicked intentions is hated. ¹⁸The simple inherit folly, But the prudent

are crowned with knowledge. ¹⁹The evil will bow before the good, And the wicked at the gates of the righteous.

²⁰The poor [man] is hated even by his own neighbor, But the rich [has] many friends. ²¹He who despises his neighbor sins; But he who has mercy on the poor, happy [is] he. ²²Do they not go astray who devise evil? But mercy and truth [belong] to those who devise good.
²³In all labor there is profit, But idle chatter [leads] only to poverty.
²⁴The crown of the wise is their riches, [But] the foolishness of fools [is] folly.

²⁵A true witness delivers souls, But a deceitful [witness] speaks lies.
²⁶In the fear of the LORD [there is] strong confidence, And His children will have a place of refuge. ²⁷The fear of the LORD [is] a fountain of life, To turn [one] away from the snares of death.
²⁸In a multitude of people [is] a king's honor, But in the lack of people [is] the downfall of a prince.
²⁹[He who is] slow to wrath has great understanding, But [he who is] impulsive exalts folly.
³⁰A sound heart [is] life to the body, But envy [is] rottenness to the bones.
³¹He who oppresses the poor reproaches his Maker, But he who honors Him has mercy on the needy.
³²The wicked is banished in his wickedness, But the righteous has a refuge in his death.
³³Wisdom rests in the heart of him who has understanding, But [what is] in the heart of fools is made known.
³⁴Righteousness exalts a nation, But sin [is] a reproach to [any] people.
³⁵The king's favor [is] toward a wise servant, But his wrath [is against] him who causes shame.

Proverbs 19

¹Better [is] the poor who walks in his integrity Than [one who is] perverse in his lips, and is a fool.

²Also it is not good [for] a soul [to be] without knowledge, And he sins who hastens with [his] feet.

³The foolishness of a man twists his way, And his heart frets against the LORD.

⁴Wealth makes many friends, But the poor is separated from his friend.

⁵A false witness will not go unpunished, And [he who] speaks lies will not escape.

⁶Many entreat the favor of the nobility, And every man [is] a friend to one who gives gifts.

⁷All the brothers of the poor hate him; How much more do his friends go far from him! He may pursue [them with] words, [yet] they abandon [him].

⁸He who gets wisdom loves his own soul; He who keeps understanding will find good.

⁹A false witness will not go unpunished, And [he who] speaks lies shall perish.

¹⁰Luxury is not fitting for a fool, Much less for a servant to rule over princes.

¹¹The discretion of a man makes him slow to anger, And his glory [is] to overlook a transgression.

¹²The king's wrath [is] like the roaring of a lion, But his favor [is] like dew on the grass.

¹³A foolish son [is] the ruin of his father, And the contentions of a wife [are] a continual dripping.

¹⁴Houses and riches [are] an inheritance from fathers, But a prudent wife [is] from the LORD.

¹⁵Laziness casts [one] into a deep sleep, And an idle person will suffer hunger.

¹⁶He who keeps the commandment keeps his soul, [But] he who is careless of his ways will die.

¹⁷He who has pity on the poor lends to the LORD, And He will pay back what he has given.

¹⁸Chasten your son while there is hope, And do not set your heart on his destruction.

¹⁹[A man of] great wrath will suffer punishment; For if you rescue [him], you will have to do it again.

²⁰Listen to counsel and receive instruction, That you may be wise in your latter days.

²¹There are many plans in a man's heart, Nevertheless the LORD's counsel--that will stand.

²²What is desired in a man is kindness, And a poor man is better than a liar.

²³The fear of the LORD [leads] to life, And [he who has it] will abide in satisfaction; He will not be visited with evil.

²⁴A lazy [man] buries his hand in the bowl, And will not so much as bring it to his mouth again.

²⁵Strike a scoffer, and the simple will become wary; Rebuke one who has understanding, [and] he will discern knowledge.

⁶He who mistreats [his] father [and] chases away [his] mother [Is] a son who causes shame and brings reproach.

²⁷Cease listening to instruction, my son, And you will stray from the words of knowledge.

²⁸A disreputable witness scorns justice, And the mouth of the wicked devours iniquity.

²⁹Judgments are prepared for scoffers, And beatings for the backs of fools.

Feeding the Spirit

Elders are responsible to model and example right behavior to the younger.

¹But as for you, speak the things which are proper for sound doctrine: ²that the older men be sober, reverent, temperate, sound in faith, in love, in patience; ³the older women likewise, that they be reverent in behavior, not slanderers, not given to much wine, teachers of good things-- ⁴that they admonish the young women to love their husbands, to love their children, ⁵[to be] discreet, chaste, homemakers, good, obedient to their own husbands, that the word of God may not be blasphemed.

⁶Likewise, exhort the young men to be sober-minded, ⁷in all things showing yourself [to be] a pattern of good works; in doctrine [showing] integrity, reverence, incorruptibility, ⁸sound speech that cannot be condemned, that one who is an opponent may be ashamed, having nothing evil to say of you. ⁹[Exhort] bondservants to be obedient to their own masters, to be well pleasing in all [things], not answering back, ¹⁰not pilfering, but showing all good fidelity, that they may adorn the doctrine of God our Savior in all things. Titus 2

Thoughts, emotions, and regret can anguish the spirit. It can be the worst of all outcomes to suffer the consequences of our own actions. Prolonged periods in the "woodshed" can drive belief to the breaking point. During low periods, immerse yourself in the Word and things of God to encourage, refresh, and strengthen resolve.

³¹But those who wait on the LORD Shall renew [their] strength; They shall mount up with wings like eagles, They shall run and not be weary, They shall walk and not faint. – Isaiah 40

Industry & Wealth

Working and honest pursuit of this worlds goods is respectable while slavish obsession with money and material possessions corrupts.

Leadership Maxims

Create an environment where talent, drive, and ingenuity are amply rewarded and exist to benefit both the individual and the aggregate.

Industry

It is impossible to motivate someone else, rather look to create incentives that spark motivation in others.

Work smarter not harder to reap the reward of well-crafted plans and diligence.

Don't overburden process with complex solutions that are over-kill. Evaluate and develop existing tools and services to more effective use rather than jumping on the bandwagon of prevailing opinion that opts for federated systems when a simple solution works best.

Failure is a signal to self-evaluate, retrench, and redirect; often there is something better ahead. Don't be hesitant to back off when outcomes are not as anticipated or optimal– never sink good money after bad. It's always best to cut losses as soon as ineffective outcomes are apparent.

Self-starters are by nature highly motivated; they are independent but need vision, let them know you support their efforts and are confident in their judgement.

When expertise and skill sets go unrecognized passive acceptance in a stifling environment affects morale, self-confidence, productivity, and willingness to problem-solve - the talent killers.

When subjected to the control of one person who is widely considered "the only authoritative voice" don't waste time, you will never penetrate or supplant perception, it's empowered above you. Controllers are in for life and will vigorously thwart any perceived threat to fiefdom.

Controllers mark themselves; they corral knowledge and make themselves the wellspring of information to whom all others must defer. The controller disregards repeatable process to maintain position making accountability and continuous improvement impossible, weakening the entire delivery chain.

Laziness manifests in indolence and lack of interest in goals or set objectives. Searching for the 'hot button' in the lackadaisical takes tenacity and frank discussion, but understand, with some nothing salves a wound; be inclusive but know when to say when.

Lazy slovenly habits are fostered by lifestyle. Generally, the more you indulge laziness the lazier you become. If lack of energy is the problem adjust your diet and exercise patterns, or consult a doctor for help.

Although the slothful are highly predicable some are driven by acrimony that can become volatile.

For most, substance abuse kills motivation, impedes progress, and distorts thinking. Slavish addictions are disabling, the robber barons of success that will rule over you.

Wealth
Be mindful of accepting gifts or help from those that will enslave you.

Greed and obsession with material wealth or coveted positions exerts unhealthy control over motivation and behavior.

Often, money is used as a means of control, with the expectation of gaining influence or an acknowledged obligation. Once accepted a bribe subjugates the receiver to the giver, you are under the power of another. Some "favors" have the same effect. Measure your need for independence; distance yourself from the obligation of owing another because of a past favor.

Keep a careful check on borrowings, it wields an oppressive control from which it is nearly impossible to escape.

How the poor are benefited. "Give a man a fish, and you feed him for a day. Teach a man to fish and you feed him for a lifetime."

The adage speaks to self-sufficiency. People empowered by economic independence are self-reliant. While charity has its place in the care of those that cannot care for themselves, creating a class of dependent, indolent, uneducated, entitled people through government imposed redistribution of wealth is destructive.

Engineered dependence is sustained generationally when empowered through lack of or deficient education, and creates a totalitarian welfare state in which greater and greater numbers of people are subjected to a slave-like existence; the antithesis of freedom.

The philosophy of the school room in one generation will be the philosophy of government in the next.
Abraham Lincoln

Proverbs 6

¹My son, if you become surety for your friend, [If] you have shaken hands in pledge for a stranger, ²You are snared by the words of your mouth; You are taken by the words of your mouth. ³So do this, my son, and deliver yourself; For you have come into the hand of your friend: Go and humble yourself; Plead with your friend. ⁴Give no sleep to your eyes, Nor slumber to your eyelids. ⁵Deliver yourself like a gazelle from the hand [of the hunter], And like a bird from the hand of the fowler.

⁶Go to the ant, you sluggard! Consider her ways and be wise, ⁷Which, having no captain, Overseer or ruler, ⁸Provides her supplies in the summer, [And] gathers her food in the harvest. ⁹How long will you slumber, O sluggard? When will you rise from your sleep? ¹⁰A little sleep, a little slumber, A little folding of the hands to sleep--¹¹So shall your poverty come on you like a prowler, And your need like an armed man.

¹²A worthless person, a wicked man, Walks with a perverse mouth; ¹³He winks with his eyes, He shuffles his feet, He points with his fingers; ¹⁴Perversity [is] in his heart, He devises evil continually, He sows discord. ¹⁵Therefore his calamity shall come suddenly; Suddenly he shall be broken without remedy.

¹⁶These six [things] the LORD hates, Yes, seven [are] an abomination to Him: ¹⁷A proud look, A lying tongue, Hands that shed innocent blood,¹⁸A heart that devises wicked plans, Feet that are swift in running to evil, ¹⁹A false witness [who] speaks lies, And one who sows discord among brethren.

²⁰My son, keep your father's command, And do not forsake the law of your mother. ²¹Bind them continually upon your heart; Tie them around your neck. ²²When you roam, they will lead you; When you sleep, they will keep you; And [when] you awake, they will speak with you. ²³For the commandment [is] a lamp, And the law a light; Reproofs of instruction [are] the way of life,²⁴To keep you from the evil woman, From the

flattering tongue of a seductress. ²⁵Do not lust after her beauty in your heart, Nor let her allure you with her eyelids. ²⁶For by means of a harlot [A man is reduced] to a crust of bread; And an adulteress will prey upon his precious life. ²⁷Can a man take fire to his bosom, And his clothes not be burned? ²⁸Can one walk on hot coals, And his feet not be seared? ²⁹So [is] he who goes in to his neighbor's wife; Whoever touches her shall not be innocent.

³⁰[People] do not despise a thief If he steals to satisfy himself when he is starving. ³¹Yet [when] he is found, he must restore sevenfold; He may have to give up all the substance of his house.

³²Whoever commits adultery with a woman lacks understanding; He [who] does so destroys his own soul. ³³Wounds and dishonor he will get, And his reproach will not be wiped away. ³⁴For jealousy [is] a husband's fury; Therefore he will not spare in the day of vengeance. ³⁵He will accept no recompense, Nor will he be appeased though you give many gifts.

Proverbs 17

¹Better [is] a dry morsel with quietness, Than a house full of feasting [with] strife.

²A wise servant will rule over a son who causes shame, And will share an inheritance among the brothers.

³The refining pot [is] for silver and the furnace for gold, But the LORD tests the hearts.

⁴An evildoer gives heed to false lips; A liar listens eagerly to a spiteful tongue.

⁵He who mocks the poor reproaches his Maker; He who is glad at calamity will not go unpunished.

⁶You shall not pervert the judgment of your poor in his dispute.

⁶Children's children [are] the crown of old men, And the glory of children [is] their father.

⁷Excellent speech is not becoming to a fool, Much less lying lips to a prince.

⁸A present [is] a precious stone in the eyes of its possessor; Wherever he turns, he prospers.

⁹He who covers a transgression seeks love, But he who repeats a matter separates friends.

¹⁰Rebuke is more effective for a wise [man] Than a hundred blows on a fool.

¹¹An evil [man] seeks only rebellion; Therefore a cruel messenger will be sent against him.

¹²Let a man meet a bear robbed of her cubs, Rather than a fool in his folly.

¹³Whoever rewards evil for good, Evil will not depart from his house.

¹⁴The beginning of strife [is like] releasing water; Therefore stop contention before a quarrel starts.

¹⁵He who justifies the wicked, and he who condemns the just, Both of them alike [are] an abomination to the LORD.

¹⁶Why [is there] in the hand of a fool the purchase price of wisdom, Since [he has] no heart [for it]?

¹⁷A friend loves at all times, And a brother is born for adversity.

¹⁸A man devoid of understanding shakes hands in a pledge, [And] becomes surety for his friend.

¹⁹He who loves transgression loves strife, And he who exalts his gate seeks destruction.

²⁰He who has a deceitful heart finds no good, And he who has a perverse tongue falls into evil.

²¹He who begets a scoffer [does so] to his sorrow, And the father of a fool has no joy.

²²A merry heart does good, [like] medicine, But a broken spirit dries the bones.

²³A wicked [man] accepts a bribe behind the back To pervert the ways of justice.

²⁴Wisdom [is] in the sight of him who has understanding, But the eyes of a fool [are] on the ends of the earth.

²⁵A foolish son [is] a grief to his father, And bitterness to her who bore him.

²⁶Also, to punish the righteous [is] not good, [Nor] to strike princes for [their] uprightness.

²⁷He who has knowledge spares his words, [And] a man of understanding is of a calm spirit.

²⁸Even a fool is counted wise when he holds his peace; [When] he shuts his lips, [he is considered] perceptive.

Proverbs 23

¹When you sit down to eat with a ruler, Consider carefully what [is] before you;²And put a knife to your throat If you [are] a man given to appetite. ³Do not desire his delicacies, For they [are] deceptive food.

⁴Do not overwork to be rich; Because of your own understanding, cease! ⁵Will you set your eyes on that which is not? For [riches] certainly make themselves wings; They fly away like an eagle [toward] heaven.

⁶Do not eat the bread of a miser, Nor desire his delicacies; ⁷For as he thinks in his heart, so [is] he. "Eat and drink!" he says to you, But his heart is not with you. ⁸The morsel you have eaten, you will vomit up, And waste your pleasant words.

⁹Do not speak in the hearing of a fool, For he will despise the wisdom of your words.
¹⁰Do not remove the ancient landmark, Nor enter the fields of the fatherless;¹¹For their Redeemer [is] mighty; He will plead their cause against you.
¹²Apply your heart to instruction, And your ears to words of knowledge.
¹³Do not withhold correction from a child, For [if] you beat him with a rod, he will not die. ¹⁴You shall beat him with a rod, And deliver his soul from hell.

¹⁵My son, if your heart is wise, My heart will rejoice--indeed, I myself; ¹⁶Yes, my inmost being will rejoice When your lips speak right things. ¹⁷Do not let your heart envy sinners, But [be zealous] for the fear of the LORD all the day; ¹⁸For surely there is a hereafter, And your hope will not be cut off.

¹⁹Hear, my son, and be wise; And guide your heart in the way. ²⁰Do not mix with winebibbers, [Or] with gluttonous eaters of

meat;²¹For the drunkard and the glutton will come to poverty, And drowsiness will clothe [a man] with rags.

²²Listen to your father who begot you, And do not despise your mother when she is old.
²³Buy the truth, and do not sell [it], [Also] wisdom and instruction and understanding.
²⁴The father of the righteous will greatly rejoice, And he who begets a wise [child] will delight in him.
²⁵Let your father and your mother be glad, And let her who bore you rejoice.

²⁶My son, give me your heart, And let your eyes observe my ways.²⁷For a harlot [is] a deep pit, And a seductress [is] a narrow well. ²⁸She also lies in wait as [for] a victim, And increases the unfaithful among men.

²⁹Who has woe? Who has sorrow? Who has contentions? Who has complaints? Who has wounds without cause? Who has redness of eyes? ³⁰Those who linger long at the wine, Those who go in search of mixed wine. ³¹Do not look on the wine when it is red, When it sparkles in the cup, [When] it swirls around smoothly; ³²At the last it bites like a serpent, And stings like a viper. ³³Your eyes will see strange things, And your heart will utter perverse things. ³⁴Yes, you will be like one who lies down in the midst of the sea, Or like one who lies at the top of the mast, [saying]: ³⁵"They have struck me, [but] I was not hurt; They have beaten me, but I did not feel [it]. When shall I awake, that I may seek another [drink]?"

Feeding the Spirit

Laziness leads to total dependence on the good will of others and is often proliferated generationally. [10]... If anyone is not willing to work, let him not eat. [11]For we hear that some among you walk in idleness, not busy at work, but busybodies. [12]Now such persons we command and encourage in the Lord Jesus Christ to do their work quietly and to earn their own living.
2 Thessalonians 3 [ESV]

If you feel compelled to meet another's financial need, give the money expecting nothing in return; but do not give what you cannot be without– it churns up regret that defeats the good work.

Seeking and obtaining wealth is a curious thing; while honest work is blessed the pursuit of riches for evil selfish reasons is never sanctioned.

[9]But those who want to be rich fall into temptation, a trap, and many foolish and harmful desires, which plunge people into ruin and destruction. [10] For the love of money is a root of all kinds of evil, and by craving it, some have wandered away from the faith and pierced themselves with many griefs. 1 Timothy 6 [CSB]

Spending patterns and desires for wealth are self alerting signals that indicate the importance and depth of our relationship with the LORD. All we possess comes from the Him, returning a portion of that which He has bestowed can be a strong indication of commitment.

[17]As for the rich in this present age, charge them not to be haughty, nor to set their hopes on the uncertainty of riches, but on God, who richly provides us with everything to enjoy. [18]They are to do good, to be rich in good works, to be generous and ready to share. 1 Timothy 6 [ESV]

Avoid the snare of the wealth web; it is a temporal happiness. We take nothing but accountability into the next life. Consider Lazarus.

[19]There was a certain rich man who was clothed in purple and fine linen and fared sumptuously every day. [20]But there was a certain beggar named Lazarus, full of sores, who was laid at his gate…

[22]So it was that the beggar died, and was carried by the angels to Abraham's bosom. The rich man also died and was buried.[23]and being in torments in Hades, he lifted up his eyes and saw Abraham afar off and Lazarus in his bosom. [24]Then he cried and said, 'Father Abraham have mercy on me and send Lazarus that he may dip the tip of his finger in water and cool my tongue for I am tormented in this flame.' [25]But Abraham said, 'Son, remember that in your lifetime you received your good things, and likewise Lazarus evil things, but now he is comforted and you are tormented. Luke 16

Plans & Deeds

Well laid plans are key to any successful venture; make the plan, man the plan, execute the plan. Our deeds have the power to outlive us, how will you be remembered?

Leadership Maxims

Regardless of what you say, your actions bear you out. Scrutinize your motives; understand the reason you choose to act or speak, particularly when harm to another is an outcome. Conformance and obedience to wrongful actions, especially those that impose life threating circumstances, and later laying claim to a "just following orders" defense, in the end, never exonerates the guilty.

While preparation and planning is key to success, it must be the right plan. Doing the wrong thing, even exceptionally well, is of no value.

Even the best plan can come to nothing in the face of entrenched opposition. Learn to view failure as a temporary setback that requires renewed efforts to pilot a more effective way forward. When faced with unyielding resistance, re-evaluate, course correct, and wait for the right moment.

Suppress erratic displays of behavior: uncontrolled outbursts, tirades laced with partial truth or spin, rendering judgement or accusation based in personality likes or dislikes. These are hard mastered disciplines that will severely challenge behavioral weaknesses and your deepest held self-image.

Don't fall in love with your own ideas. The "not invented here" mentality constricts intuitive thinkers and shackles the possible.

If you lack organizational skills make team resource selections that will compensate for the void and empower corrective actions. Organizing and deploying resources, information, and data, are foundational to decision making.

Monitor and measure professional risk; choose battles and timing carefully. Advancing opposition to wrongful courses of action in mid-execution takes tremendous conviction and courage. When position overrules economy and good sense it is unlikely sound reasoning will prevail. Crisis points can provide opportunity to voice persuasive opposition. Winning converts helps turn the tide.

That which you endorse and actively support reveals your resolve to stand for the right. Policy is no substitute for accountability. Choosing rule by committee is reserved for the cowardly, those unwilling to accept responsibility for outcomes.

Resorting to tactics of personal destruction against another, especially an opponent, signals a lack of substance that supports position. Use facts to strengthen argument, never resort to personal attacks.

Making right an inflicted wrong is a mark of personal integrity and sincerity that inspires trust.

Change is a life constant and is imposed for a plurality of reasons. Its effects can be varied, but regardless of stated outcomes most people resist change. Help the resistant embrace the inevitable, acknowledge what is true but focus on creating positive outcomes.

Excuses that cover indecision and inaction are common traits in those that shirk responsibility for outcomes. It's the ability to grasp circumstances, sense the motives of others, and rightly anticipate future events that sets you apart from the mediocre.

Take the A^2F^2 Challenge. Measure yourself against behaviors that are backed by positive action, not mere lip service.

Accountability:

- Do you subordinate personality likes and dislikes to standards of impartiality?
- Do you repeat the company line to protect yourself?
- Do you stand firm for the right and take ownership of outcomes?
- Do you back off courses of action that prove ineffective?
- Do you admit when you have been wrong?
- Is your memory of events accurate?
- Are you erratic in thought and communication sending mixed or unclear messages that confuse and befuddle?
- Are you mindful of the effects your decisions impose on others?
- In situations where communication is breaking down, are you the mediator that bridges the gap?

Availability:
- How is your "open-door policy" used; as brow-beating submission sessions or opportunities for objective learning?
- Do you listen with empathy, walking a mile in the other guy's shoes?
- Are you attentive to and remember from whence you came; thinking back, reflecting on your own experiences.
- Adhering to chain of command rules and creating an atmosphere of equity and candor is a precarious balance. Opening channels of unencumbered communication in a bottom-up framework can be enlightening, you will undoubtedly hear all from every viewpoint, some of which will be profitable.

Feasibility:
- Will outcomes serve as a win-win to those affected by them?
- Is the objective realistic by standards of the environment?
- Is there a dependable supporting coalition that will help rather than hinder, or worse, adversely or openly oppose?
- Is it technically achievable within scope and budget constraints. Is there a reliable proof of concept?

Flexibility:
- Do you embrace needful change or do you keep doing the same thing expecting a different result.
- Are you willing to change course based on reliable information?
- Are you an idea killer that shuts down exchanges because they weren't "invented here."
- Are you open to the opinions and ideas of others, regardless of position or perceived importance in the organization?
- Are you on the scout for and recognize idea generators?

Proverbs 21

¹The king's heart [is] in the hand of the LORD, [Like] the rivers of water; He turns it wherever He wishes.
²Every way of a man [is] right in his own eyes, But the LORD weighs the hearts. ³To do righteousness and justice [Is] more acceptable to the LORD than sacrifice.

⁴A haughty look, a proud heart, [And] the plowing of the wicked [are] sin.
⁵The plans of the diligent [lead] surely to plenty, But [those of] everyone [who is] hasty, surely to poverty.
⁶Getting treasures by a lying tongue [Is] the fleeting fantasy of those who seek death.
⁷The violence of the wicked will destroy them, Because they refuse to do justice.
⁸The way of a guilty man [is] perverse; But [as for] the pure, his work [is] right.
⁹Better to dwell in a corner of a housetop, Than in a house shared with a contentious woman.
¹⁰The soul of the wicked desires evil; His neighbor finds no favor in his eyes.
¹¹When the scoffer is punished, the simple is made wise; But when the wise is instructed, he receives knowledge.
¹²The righteous [God] wisely considers the house of the wicked, Overthrowing the wicked for [their] wickedness.
¹³Whoever shuts his ears to the cry of the poor Will also cry himself and not be heard.
¹⁴A gift in secret pacifies anger, And a bribe behind the back, strong wrath.
¹⁵[It is] a joy for the just to do justice, But destruction [will come] to the workers of iniquity.
¹⁶A man who wanders from the way of understanding Will rest in the assembly of the dead.
¹⁷He who loves pleasure [will be] a poor man; He who loves wine and oil will not be rich.
¹⁸The wicked [shall be] a ransom for the righteous, And the unfaithful for the upright.

¹⁹Better to dwell in the wilderness, Than with a contentious and angry woman.

²⁰[There is] desirable treasure, And oil in the dwelling of the wise, But a foolish man squanders it.

²¹He who follows righteousness and mercy Finds life, righteousness, and honor.

²²A wise [man] scales the city of the mighty, And brings down the trusted stronghold.

²³Whoever guards his mouth and tongue Keeps his soul from troubles.

²⁴A proud [and] haughty [man]--"Scoffer" [is] his name; He acts with arrogant pride.

²⁵The desire of the lazy [man] kills him, For his hands refuse to labor. ²⁶He covets greedily all day long, But the righteous gives and does not spare.

²⁷The sacrifice of the wicked [is] an abomination; How much more [when] he brings it with wicked intent!

²⁸A false witness shall perish, But the man who hears [him] will speak endlessly.

²⁹A wicked man hardens his face, But [as for] the upright, he establishes his way.

³⁰[There is] no wisdom or understanding Or counsel against the LORD.

³¹The horse [is] prepared for the day of battle, But deliverance [is] of the LORD.

Proverbs 28

¹The wicked flee when no one pursues, But the righteous are bold as a lion.

²Because of the transgression of a land, many [are] its princes; But by a man of understanding [and] knowledge Right will be prolonged.

³A poor man who oppresses the poor [Is like] a driving rain which leaves no food.

⁴Those who forsake the law praise the wicked, But such as keep the law contend with them.

⁵Evil men do not understand justice, But those who seek the LORD understand all.

⁶Better [is] the poor who walks in his integrity Than one perverse [in his] ways, though he [be] rich.

⁷Whoever keeps the law [is] a discerning son, But a companion of gluttons shames his father.

⁸One who increases his possessions by usury and extortion Gathers it for him who will pity the poor.

⁹One who turns away his ear from hearing the law, Even his prayer [is] an abomination.

¹⁰Whoever causes the upright to go astray in an evil way, He himself will fall into his own pit; But the blameless will inherit good.

¹¹The rich man [is] wise in his own eyes, But the poor who has understanding searches him out.

¹²When the righteous rejoice, [there is] great glory; But when the wicked arise, men hide themselves.

¹³He who covers his sins will not prosper, But whoever confesses and forsakes [them] will have mercy.

¹⁴Happy [is] the man who is always reverent, But he who hardens his heart will fall into calamity.

¹⁵[Like] a roaring lion and a charging bear [Is] a wicked ruler over poor people.

¹⁶A ruler who lacks understanding [is] a great oppressor, [But] he who hates covetousness will prolong [his] days.

¹⁷A man burdened with bloodshed will flee into a pit; Let no one help him.

¹⁸Whoever walks blamelessly will be saved, But [he who is] perverse [in his] ways will suddenly fall.

¹⁹He who tills his land will have plenty of bread, But he who follows frivolity will have poverty enough!

²⁰A faithful man will abound with blessings, But he who hastens to be rich will not go unpunished.

²¹To show partiality [is] not good, Because for a piece of bread a man will transgress.

²²A man with an evil eye hastens after riches, And does not consider that poverty will come upon him.

²³He who rebukes a man will find more favor afterward Than he who flatters with the tongue.

²⁴Whoever robs his father or his mother, And says, "[It is] no transgression," The same [is] companion to a destroyer.

²⁵He who is of a proud heart stirs up strife, But he who trusts in the LORD will be prospered.

²⁶He who trusts in his own heart is a fool, But whoever walks wisely will be delivered.

²⁷He who gives to the poor will not lack, But he who hides his eyes will have many curses.

²⁸When the wicked arise, men hide themselves; But when they perish, the righteous increase.

Proverbs 29

¹He who is often rebuked, [and] hardens [his] neck, Will suddenly be destroyed, and that without remedy.

²When the righteous are in authority, the people rejoice; But when a wicked [man] rules, the people groan.

³Whoever loves wisdom makes his father rejoice, But a companion of harlots wastes [his] wealth.

⁴The king establishes the land by justice, But he who receives bribes overthrows it.

⁵A man who flatters his neighbor Spreads a net for his feet.

⁶By transgression an evil man is snared, But the righteous sings and rejoices.

⁷The righteous considers the cause of the poor, [But] the wicked does not understand [such] knowledge.

⁸Scoffers set a city aflame, But wise [men] turn away wrath.

⁹[If] a wise man contends with a foolish man, Whether [the fool] rages or laughs, [there is] no peace.

¹⁰The bloodthirsty hate the blameless, But the upright seek his well-being.

¹¹A fool vents all his feelings, But a wise [man] holds them back.

¹²If a ruler pays attention to lies, All his servants [become] wicked.

¹³The poor [man] and the oppressor have this in common: The LORD gives light to the eyes of both.

¹⁴The king who judges the poor with truth, His throne will be established forever.

¹⁵The rod and rebuke give wisdom, But a child left [to himself] brings shame to his mother.

¹⁶When the wicked are multiplied, transgression increases; But the righteous will see their fall.

¹⁷Correct your son, and he will give you rest; Yes, he will give delight to your soul.

¹⁸Where [there is] no revelation, the people cast off restraint; But happy [is] he who keeps the law.

¹⁹A servant will not be corrected by mere words; For though he understands, he will not respond.

²⁰Do you see a man hasty in his words? [There is] more hope for a fool than for him.

²¹He who pampers his servant from childhood Will have him as a son in the end.

²²An angry man stirs up strife, And a furious man abounds in transgression.

²³A man's pride will bring him low, But the humble in spirit will retain honor.

²⁴Whoever is a partner with a thief hates his own life; He swears to tell the truth, but reveals nothing.

²⁵The fear of man brings a snare, But whoever trusts in the LORD shall be safe.

²⁶Many seek the ruler's favor, But justice for man [comes] from the LORD.

²⁷An unjust man [is] an abomination to the righteous, And [he who is] upright in the way [is] an abomination to the wicked.

Feeding the Spirit

Petition the Lord, prayerfully bring all your plans, aspirations, and disappointments to Him. Trust that Our Lord acts and orders events in our best interests even in the face of what appears to be total defeat. *[6] Be anxious for nothing, but in everything by prayer and supplication, with thanksgiving, let your requests be made known to God... Philippians 4* Settle this in your mind: the Lord will keep us from that which is hurtful when the object of our goal or affection is injurious.

Standards of right and wrong are rooted in the Word God. Since Eden humanity has been subject to sin, but to rule over our sin nature separates us from evil. Remember our LORD's admonition to Cain. *[7]If you do what is right, will you not be accepted? But if you refuse to do what is right, sin is crouching at your door; it desires you, but you must master it. Genesis 4 [BSB]*

Your worth and integrity may go unnoticed, but at the end of the day you can, with assurance, rest in the knowledge when you do no harm; you did not undermine or connive the downfall of another. Remember you are *[16]...as sheep in the midst of wolves. Therefore be wise as serpents and harmless as doves. Matthew 1*

The act of acknowledging wrongdoing may not be meaningful to the hearer, but it honors and is known by the Lord. Regardless of what others may think, say, or do, make right, as much as it is in your power, any wrong you have inflicted on others.

Forced compliance to less than upright methods is never acceptable; do not scruple, turn away without regret. [5]And if a town refuses to welcome you, shake its dust from your feet as you leave to show that you have abandoned those people to their fate. Luke 9 [NLT]

Consider this carefully, accountability is applied individually, each of us answers before the LORD for themselves. [10] For we must all appear before the judgment seat of Christ, so that each one may receive what is due for what he has done in the body, whether good or evil. Corinthians 5 (ESV)

The hardest thing of all: leave retribution to the Lord, [9]But even when Michael the archangel was arguing with the devil and debating with him concerning Moses' body, he did not dare to bring a slanderous judgment, but said, "May the Lord rebuke you!" Jude 1 [CSB]

Seduction

Invitations of a sexual nature will always be within your grasp to accept, regardless of gender. You are the determiner of your own actions.

Leadership Maxims

Engaging in intimate relations with those in your charge risks losing the respect and love of your family, sullying your reputation in the workplace, reducing your peer standing to an object of ridicule and gossip, and in some cases may reach the level of legal prosecution. This is much to sacrifice for an unguarded moment. Your own conviction must form the foundation of acceptable behavior.

Understand this: perception becomes truth. We cannot be responsible for every snide remark motivated by jealousy or bitterness, but we can guard against providing fodder for the rumor mill.

The immoral lurk everywhere and entice through allurements and provocative banter. Train yourself to keep attractions of a sexual nature under a well-controlled wrap. The temptation to exploit another sexually in the midst of what is freely offered can be overwhelming. If/when you feel vulnerable, pull away; do not submit yourself to situations that weaken resolve.

You will be distanced from harming others and yourself when you are clear of interests that use, abuse, molest, and/or sexually injure others.

Abuses that control and dominate behavior render you useless to yourself and others. Be wise and like Pandora's box do not release what could become uncontrollable.

Flattery is seductive, learn to distinguish true admiration vice adulation meant to cultivate an alliance.

Proverbs 5

¹My son, pay attention to my wisdom; Lend your ear to my understanding, ²That you may preserve discretion, And your lips may keep knowledge.

³For the lips of an immoral woman drip honey, And her mouth [is] smoother than oil; ⁴But in the end she is bitter as wormwood, Sharp as a two-edged sword. ⁵Her feet go down to death, Her steps lay hold of hell. ⁶Lest you ponder [her] path of life--Her ways are unstable; You do not know [them].

⁷Therefore hear me now, [my] children, And do not depart from the words of my mouth. ⁸Remove your way far from her, And do not go near the door of her house, ⁹Lest you give your honor to others, And your years to the cruel [one]; ¹⁰Lest aliens be filled with your wealth, And your labors [go] to the house of a foreigner;¹¹And you mourn at last, When your flesh and your body are consumed, ¹²And say: "How I have hated instruction, And my heart despised correction! ¹³I have not obeyed the voice of my teachers, Nor inclined my ear to those who instructed me! ¹⁴I was on the verge of total ruin, In the midst of the assembly and congregation."

¹⁵Drink water from your own cistern, And running water from your own well. ¹⁶Should your fountains be dispersed abroad, Streams of water in the streets? ¹⁷Let them be only your own, And not for strangers with you. ¹⁸Let your fountain be blessed, And rejoice with the wife of your youth. ¹⁹[As a] loving deer and a graceful doe, Let her breasts satisfy you at all times; And always be enraptured with her love. ²⁰For why should you, my son, be enraptured by an immoral woman, And be embraced in the arms of a seductress? ²¹For the ways of man [are] before the eyes of the LORD, And He ponders all his paths.

²²His own iniquities entrap the wicked [man], And he is caught in the cords of his sin. ²³He shall die for lack of instruction, And in the greatness of his folly he shall go astray.

Proverbs 7

[1]My son, keep my words, And treasure my commands within you. [2]Keep my commands and live, And my law as the apple of your eye. [3]Bind them on your fingers; Write them on the tablet of your heart. [4]Say to wisdom, "You [are] my sister," And call understanding [your] nearest kin, [5]That they may keep you from the immoral woman, From the seductress [who] flatters with her words.

[6]For at the window of my house I looked through my lattice, [7]And saw among the simple, I perceived among the youths, A young man devoid of understanding, [8]Passing along the street near her corner; And he took the path to her house [9]In the twilight, in the evening, In the black and dark night. [10]And there a woman met him, [With] the attire of a harlot, and a crafty heart. [11]She [was] loud and rebellious, Her feet would not stay at home. [12]At times [she was] outside, at times in the open square, Lurking at every corner. [13]So she caught him and kissed him; With an impudent face she said to him:[14]"[I have] peace offerings with me; Today I have paid my vows. [15]So I came out to meet you, Diligently to seek your face, And I have found you. [16]I have spread my bed with tapestry, Colored coverings of Egyptian linen. [17]I have perfumed my bed With myrrh, aloes, and cinnamon. [18]Come, let us take our fill of love until morning; Let us delight ourselves with love. [19]For my husband [is] not at home; He has gone on a long journey; [20]He has taken a bag of money with him, [And] will come home on the appointed day."

[21]With her enticing speech she caused him to yield, With her flattering lips she seduced him. [22]Immediately he went after her, as an ox goes to the slaughter, Or as a fool to the correction of the stocks,[23]Till an arrow struck his liver. As a bird hastens to the snare, He did not know it [would cost] his life.

[24]Now therefore, listen to me, [my] children; Pay attention to the words of my mouth: [25]Do not let your heart turn aside to

her ways, Do not stray into her paths; [26]For she has cast down many wounded, And all who were slain by her were strong [men]. [27]Her house [is] the way to hell, Descending to the chambers of death.

Feeding the Spirit

Obsessive carnal appetites bring slavish subjection to behaviors that lack self-control. Filling your thoughts with sensual fantasies can lead to behavior from which it is hard to pull free. Once the mind settles a matter we are less sensitive to the rebuke of conscience and with the passing of time its warnings are not heard at all.

Wisdom is personified throughout the Proverbs in the feminine. She contrasts sharply with the foolish boisterous woman that exploits one quality only, sex appeal.

Solomon speaks openly about sexual seduction. He knew well the addictive nature of unrestrained sexual passion. We live in social circumstances of unlimited prurient urges – any sexual conduct passes as acceptable.

Human sexuality is a God given gift designed for pleasure, satisfaction, and procreation. Strive to keep your sexual desires within the bonds of marriage; once married do all in your power to meet the desires of your spouse.

[2]Oh, that he would kiss me with the kisses of his mouth! For your caresses are more delightful than wine. ...[3]The fragrance of your perfume is pleasing; your name is like perfume poured out. No wonder the maidens adore you. [13]The one I love is a sachet of myrrh to me, spending the night between my breasts. ... [16]How handsome you are, my beloved! Oh, how delightful! The soft grass is our bed. Song of Solomon 1 [CSB]

[1]How beautiful you are, my darling—how very beautiful! Your eyes are like doves behind your veil. [3]Your lips are like a scarlet ribbon, and your mouth is lovely. [7]You are altogether beautiful, my darling; in you there is no flaw. [9]You have captured my heart, my sister, my bride; you have stolen my heart with one glance of your eyes, with one jewel of your neck.[10]How delightful is your love, my sister, my bride! Your

love is much better than wine, and the fragrance of your perfume than all spices. Song of Solomon 4 [CSB]

The Wicked

Beliefs define core values; core values shape character traits and permissible latitudes of behavior. Acts that demonstrate an imprudent lack of self-control, an unconscienced disregard for others, envy, jealousy, deceit, and malicious intent are conduct of the wicked.

Leadership Maxims

Wickedness is evidenced by habitual behaviors: spreading dissension, furthering malicious gossip, lying about or misrepresenting situations or persons, backbiting, bitterness, hatred toward innocence, prideful arrogance, jealousy, envy, covetousness. Guard against these character traits in yourself and keep away from those that show themselves captive to such behaviors.

Recognize the rash and pernicious in your midst. Self-centered and self-serving obsessions are traits of the wicked. When consistent behaviors indicate the sole concern with self be on your guard.

Do not stand with or be counted among those that devise or plot harm to others. Influence is subtle; surroundings have power to desensitize. Peer and organizational pressure can lead to wrongdoing that sullies reputation.

Regulate your thoughts in times of extreme stress, chaos, and crisis. Short, intemperate responses betray a lack of self-control and forethought. Monitor conversation so as not to stir-up anger or resentment in others. Word wounds have long memories; once said, a thing cannot be un-said.

Those that successfully govern temper have a calming influence. Proper anger management is a great benefit personally and serves as a model to others; strive to keep issues of temper under proper control.

As wicked leadership is the bane of nations, so it is with organizations. Those in leadership are held to a higher standard of accountability because they exert power over circumstances and people. In the righteous this is humbling; they know they are answerable for their actions.

Evil

Evil can be subtle and when nurtured in the heart rules the mind and justifies behavior. Any preemptive, vengeful, or retaliatory act is deemed acceptable to gain an end. Being absorbed in abusive vices is the mark of iniquity and should not be named in a leader. Be circumspect, scrutinize motives, it's easy to justify wrongful actions when emotions, self-centeredness, or greed rules.

Right thinking directs and delivers while evil ensnares and traps the doer. Contention, argument, ill-will, and deception are provinces of evil; distance yourself from worldly influences and wickedness.

Consider your name (aka reputation) in all that you do; liars, cheats, no-loads, and users are abhorred above even the mediocre. Once gained bad repute follows relentlessly. *¹A good name [is] better than precious ointment, Ecclesiastes 7*

The temptation to use a situation to benefit yourself can suppress right judgement when you have the power to manipulate circumstances. Your actions have an amazing quality of rebounding, so have a care if you are prone to harming others.

Where there is no commitment to truth any lie or deception will serve to advance an objective, purpose, or agenda. Distance yourself from those that prove themselves less than truthful and trustworthy.

Placing any degree of trust or authority in a known liar is foolhardy. The conscience of the liar has been so seared they see nothing amiss with their actions and will resort to any digression that deflects accountability. When exposed the liar maintains the fiction even as the narrative becomes ridiculous and twists in endless circles of nonsense. Casting blame on others and straying from the point are diversionary tactics; when distraction fails temper flairs.

Liars are unprincipled with intent; they revels in causing discord and misrepresenting situations or persons. They are without conscience and possess the unhappy quality of "taking in others" without remorse.

Casting affairs or events in ways that misrepresent or distort is lying. Those that resort to spin have ulterior motives that are self-serving and lack substantive evidence to prove a point. Dissention, fueled by rumormongering, is often cloaked in the guise of concern.

Foolishness
The fool rejects instruction and will not be led by sound advice. They lead others in destruction without conscience or remorse.

Fools demonstrate, with stunning regularity, a lack of discernment injecting opinion on matters about which they know little or nothing.

The simple minded wreak havoc, spew nonsense, despise correction, and see nothing amiss in themselves. The fool has no time for reflection and sees no value in pondering events, lessons learned, or sound advice.

Stubbornness demonstrated in refusal to acknowledge known facts about people and circumstance is foolish. Be, to the greatest extent possible, objectively aware of all that surrounds you.

Proverbs 10

¹The proverbs of Solomon: A wise son makes a glad father, But a foolish son [is] the grief of his mother.
²Treasures of wickedness profit nothing, But righteousness delivers from death.
³The LORD will not allow the righteous soul to famish, But He casts away the desire of the wicked.

⁴He who has a slack hand becomes poor, But the hand of the diligent makes rich.
⁵He who gathers in summer [is] a wise son; He who sleeps in harvest [is] a son who causes shame.

⁶Blessings [are] on the head of the righteous, But violence covers the mouth of the wicked.
⁷The memory of the righteous [is] blessed, But the name of the wicked will rot.
⁸The wise in heart will receive commands, But a prating fool will fall.
⁹He who walks with integrity walks securely, But he who perverts his ways will become known.
¹⁰He who winks with the eye causes trouble, But a prating fool will fall.
¹¹The mouth of the righteous [is] a well of life, But violence covers the mouth of the wicked.
¹²Hatred stirs up strife, But love covers all sins.
¹³Wisdom is found on the lips of him who has understanding, But a rod [is] for the back of him who is devoid of understanding.

¹⁴Wise [people] store up knowledge, But the mouth of the foolish [is] near destruction.
¹⁵The rich man's wealth [is] his strong city; The destruction of the poor [is] their poverty.
¹⁶The labor of the righteous [leads] to life, The wages of the wicked to sin.

¹⁷He who keeps instruction [is in] the way of life, But he who refuses correction goes astray.

¹⁸Whoever hides hatred [has] lying lips, And whoever spreads slander [is] a fool.

¹⁹In the multitude of words sin is not lacking, But he who restrains his lips [is] wise.

²⁰The tongue of the righteous [is] choice silver; The heart of the wicked [is worth] little.

²¹The lips of the righteous feed many, But fools die for lack of wisdom.

²²The blessing of the LORD makes [one] rich, And He adds no sorrow with it.

²³To do evil [is] like sport to a fool, But a man of understanding has wisdom.²⁴The fear of the wicked will come upon him, And the desire of the righteous will be granted.

²⁵When the whirlwind passes by, the wicked [is] no [more], But the righteous [has] an everlasting foundation.

²⁶As vinegar to the teeth and smoke to the eyes, So [is] the lazy [man] to those who send him.

²⁷The fear of the LORD prolongs days, But the years of the wicked will be shortened.

²⁸The hope of the righteous [will be] gladness, But the expectation of the wicked will perish.

²⁹The way of the LORD [is] strength for the upright, But destruction [will come] to the workers of iniquity.

³⁰The righteous will never be removed, But the wicked will not inhabit the earth.

³¹The mouth of the righteous brings forth wisdom, But the perverse tongue will be cut out.

³²The lips of the righteous know what is acceptable, But the mouth of the wicked [what is] perverse.

Proverbs 12

¹Whoever loves instruction loves knowledge, But he who hates correction [is] stupid.

²A good [man] obtains favor from the LORD, But a man of wicked intentions He will condemn.

³A man is not established by wickedness, But the root of the righteous cannot be moved.

⁴An excellent wife [is] the crown of her husband, But she who causes shame [is] like rottenness in his bones.

⁵The thoughts of the righteous [are] right, [But] the counsels of the
wicked [are] deceitful.

⁶The words of the wicked [are], "Lie in wait for blood," But the mouth of the upright will deliver them.

⁷The wicked are overthrown and [are] no more, But the house of the righteous will stand.

⁸A man will be commended according to his wisdom, But he who is of a perverse heart will be despised.

⁹Better [is the one] who is slighted but has a servant, Than he who honors himself but lacks bread.

¹⁰A righteous [man] regards the life of his animal, But the tender mercies of the wicked [are] cruel.

¹¹He who tills his land will be satisfied with bread, But he who follows frivolity [is] devoid of understanding.

¹²The wicked covet the catch of evil [men], But the root of the righteous yields [fruit].

¹³The wicked is ensnared by the transgression of [his] lips, But the righteous will come through trouble.

¹⁴A man will be satisfied with good by the fruit of [his] mouth, And the recompense of a man's hands will be rendered to him.

¹⁵The way of a fool [is] right in his own eyes, But he who heeds counsel [is] wise.

¹⁶A fool's wrath is known at once, But a prudent [man] covers shame.

¹⁷He [who] speaks truth declares righteousness, But a false witness, deceit.

18There is one who speaks like the piercings of a sword, But the tongue of the wise [promotes] health.

19The truthful lip shall be established forever, But a lying tongue [is] but for a moment.
20Deceit is in the heart of those who devise evil, But counselors of peace have joy.
21No grave trouble will overtake the righteous, But the wicked shall be filled with evil.
22Lying lips [are] an abomination to the LORD, But those who deal truthfully [are] His delight. 23A prudent man conceals knowledge, But the heart of fools proclaims foolishness.

24The hand of the diligent will rule, But the lazy [man] will be put to forced labor.
25Anxiety in the heart of man causes depression, But a good word makes it glad.
26The righteous should choose his friends carefully, For the way of the wicked leads them astray.
27The lazy [man] does not roast what he took in hunting, But diligence [is] man's precious possession.

28In the way of righteousness [is] life, And in [its] pathway [there is] no death.

Proverbs 20

¹Wine [is] a mocker, Strong drink [is] a brawler, And whoever is led astray by it is not wise.

²The wrath of a king [is] like the roaring of a lion; [Whoever] provokes him to anger sins [against] his own life.

³[It is] honorable for a man to stop striving, Since any fool can start a quarrel.

⁴The lazy [man] will not plow because of winter; He will beg during harvest and [have] nothing.

⁵Counsel in the heart of man [is like] deep water, But a man of understanding will draw it out.

⁶Most men will proclaim each his own goodness, But who can find a faithful man?

⁷The righteous [man] walks in his integrity; His children [are] blessed after him.

⁸A king who sits on the throne of judgment Scatters all evil with his eyes.

⁹Who can say, "I have made my heart clean, I am pure from my sin"?

¹⁰Diverse weights [and] diverse measures, They [are] both alike, an abomination to the LORD.

¹¹Even a child is known by his deeds, Whether what he does [is] pure and right.

¹²The hearing ear and the seeing eye, The LORD has made them both.

¹³Do not love sleep, lest you come to poverty; Open your eyes, [and] you will be satisfied with bread.

¹⁴"[It is] good for nothing," cries the buyer; But when he has gone his way, then he boasts.

¹⁵There is gold and a multitude of rubies, But the lips of knowledge [are] a precious jewel.

¹⁶Take the garment of one who is surety [for] a stranger, And hold it as a pledge [when it] is for a seductress.

¹⁷Bread gained by deceit [is] sweet to a man, But afterward his mouth will be filled with gravel.

¹⁸Plans are established by counsel; By wise counsel wage war.

¹⁹He who goes about [as] a talebearer reveals secrets; Therefore do not associate with one who flatters with his lips.

²⁰Whoever curses his father or his mother, His lamp will be put out in deep darkness.

²¹An inheritance gained hastily at the beginning Will not be blessed at the end.

²²Do not say, "I will recompense evil"; Wait for the LORD, and He will save you.

²³Diverse weights [are] an abomination to the LORD, And dishonest scales [are] not good.

²⁴A man's steps [are] of the LORD; How then can a man understand his own way?

²⁵[It is] a snare for a man to devote rashly [something as] holy, And afterward to reconsider [his] vows.

²⁶A wise king sifts out the wicked, And brings the threshing wheel over them.

²⁷The spirit of a man [is] the lamp of the LORD, Searching all the inner depths of his heart.

²⁸Mercy and truth preserve the king, And by lovingkindness he upholds his throne.

²⁹The glory of young men [is] their strength, And the splendor of old men [is] their gray head.

³⁰Blows that hurt cleanse away evil, As [do] stripes the inner depths of the heart.

Proverbs 26

¹As snow in summer and rain in harvest, So honor is not fitting for a fool.

²Like a flitting sparrow, like a flying swallow, So a curse without cause shall not alight.

³A whip for the horse, A bridle for the donkey, And a rod for the fool's back.⁴Do not answer a fool according to his folly, Lest you also be like him.

⁵Answer a fool according to his folly, Lest he be wise in his own eyes.

⁶He who sends a message by the hand of a fool Cuts off [his own] feet [and] drinks violence.⁷[Like] the legs of the lame that hang limp [Is] a proverb in the mouth of fools.

⁸Like one who binds a stone in a sling [Is] he who gives honor to a fool.

⁹[Like] a thorn [that] goes into the hand of a drunkard [Is] a proverb in the mouth of fools.

¹⁰The great [God] who formed everything Gives the fool [his] hire and the transgressor [his] wages.

¹¹As a dog returns to his own vomit, [So] a fool repeats his folly.

¹²Do you see a man wise in his own eyes? [There is] more hope for a fool than for him.

¹³The lazy [man] says, "[There is] a lion in the road! A fierce lion [is] in the streets!" ¹⁴[As] a door turns on its hinges, So [does] the lazy [man] on his bed. ¹⁵The lazy [man] buries his hand in the bowl; It wearies him to bring it back to his mouth.

¹⁶The lazy [man is] wiser in his own eyes Than seven men who can answer sensibly.

¹⁷He who passes by [and] meddles in a quarrel not his own [Is like] one who takes a dog by the ears.

¹⁸Like a madman who throws firebrands, arrows, and death,¹⁹[Is] the man [who] deceives his neighbor, And says, "I was only joking!"

²⁰Where [there is] no wood, the fire goes out; And where [there is] no talebearer, strife ceases. ²¹[As] charcoal [is] to burning coals, and wood to fire, So [is] a contentious man to kindle

strife. ²²The words of a talebearer [are] like tasty trifles, And they go down into the inmost body.

²³Fervent lips with a wicked heart [Are like] earthenware covered with silver dross.

²⁴He who hates, disguises [it] with his lips, And lays up deceit within himself; ²⁵When he speaks kindly, do not believe him, For [there are] seven abominations in his heart; ²⁶[Though his] hatred is covered by deceit, His wickedness will be revealed before the assembly.

²⁷Whoever digs a pit will fall into it, And he who rolls a stone will have it roll back on him.

²⁸A lying tongue hates [those who are] crushed by it, And a flattering mouth works ruin.

Feeding the Spirit

Right thinking directs and delivers while evil ensnares and traps the doer. Regardless of outward appearances wickedness, in the end, reaps only wrath.

The temptation to use a situation to benefit yourself can suppress right judgement when you have the power to manipulate circumstances.

[10]For "He who would love life And see good days, Let him refrain his tongue from evil, And his lips from speaking deceit. [11]Let him turn away from evil and do good; Let him seek peace and pursue it. 1 Peter 3

Distance yourself from evil. Repeated exposure to the unprincipled desensitizes the conscience. When the conscience is seared penetration is unlikely.

Only the fool denigrates, belittles, and denies the existence of God. Psalm 14:1...*The fool has said in his heart, "[There is] no God."* ... Evidence of His existence and intelligent design surrounds us in nature, biology, archeology, geology, and the universe itself.

Hate has become a scornful notion but the abhorrent should be hated and shunned: displays of superiority that seek to elevate above others; habitual lying without remorse, killing the innocent, contriving and carrying out evil plans, stirring up family strife.

Lies that cause irreparable damage and hurt to others are rarely forgotten. Place no reliance on the words or deeds of a liar. *[2]Deliver my soul, O LORD, from lying lips, and from a deceitful tongue. Psalm 120*

Liars are among the most abhorred people; the conscience is seared by self-deluded propriety. Habitual lying is the destroyer of all trust and among the worst of all character defects. Curb this sin with the utmost vigor it has destructive power that is unremitting.

[44] ... He [the devil] was a murderer from the beginning, and does not stand in the truth, because there is no truth in him. When he lies, he speaks out of his own character, for he is a liar and the father of lies. John 8 [ESV]

End Notes

[i] Joseph Bio-Short Resources
1) *The Holy Bible*, NKJV Genesis Chapters 37, 39-50
2) *Blue Letter Bible*, Encyclopedias/Dictionaries-Topic: Joseph

[ii] Moses Bio-Short Resources
1) **The Holy Bible,** New King James version Books: Exodus, Acts
2) *Moses (Biblical leader)*. i. Title. ii. Series: Swindoll, Charles R. Great lives from God's word. 1999 Thomas Nelson Publisher
3) *The Torah-com*. Moses the Midianite, Dr. Rabbi Tzemah Yoreh
4) Britannica. Web Page: Moses
5) Web Page: Antiquities of the Jews, Flavius Josephus - Books II and III

[iii] Solomon Bio Short Resources
1) The Holy Bible, (NKJV) Books: 1&2 Samuel, 1 Kings, 1&2 Chronicles
2) Blue Letter Bible, Easton's Bible Dictionary- Topic: Solomon
3) The Temple, It's Ministry and Services, Kindle Edition. Alfred Edersheim
4) Bible Hub. Topical Bible, Search term: King Solomon

[iv] Queen Esther Bio-Short Resources
1) The Holy Bible, NKJV. Book: Esther
2) Blue Letter Bible, Easton's Bible Dictionary- Topic: Esther
3) Bible Hub. Topical Bible, Search term: Esther

[v] Deborah Bio-Short Resources
1) The Holy Bible, NKJV. Book: Judges Chapters 4 & 5

2) *Jamieson, Fausset, and Brown's Commentary on the Whole Bible*, Kindle Edition. Rev. Robert Jamieson, D.D.; Rev. A.R. Fausset, A. M.; Rev. David Brown, D.D.
3) Bible Hub. Topical Bible, Search term: Deborah prophetess

vi George Washington Bio-Short Resources
1) George Washington, The Founding Father, Kindle Edition. Paul Johnson
2) *The Life of George Washington,* Kindle Edition. John Marshall
3) *George Washington, Volumes 4 and 5*, Audible Edition. Douglas Southall Freeman
4) *Washington's Spies,* Audible Edition. Alexander Rose.

vii William Wilberforce Bio-Short Resources
1) A Practical View of the Prevailing Religious System of Professed Christians in the Higher and Middle Classes in this Country, Kindle Edition. William Wilberforce
2) *Amazing Grace*, Kindle Edition. John Piper
3) *William Wilberforce*, Wikipedia.
4) Amazing Grace, 2006 biographical drama. Director: Michael Apted

viii Abraham Lincoln Bio-Short Resources
1) *Abraham Lincoln Speeches and Writings,* Audible Edition. Abrahma Lincoln, James Madison, Thomas Jefferson
2) *Team of Rivals,* Kindle Edition. Doris Kearns Goodwin
3) Lincoln, Historical drama 2012. Dreamworks II Distribution Co. LLC. Director: Steven Spielberg

ix Feeding the Spirit - The Heart

1) *The Essential Works of John Flavel,* Kindle Edition. John Flavel GLH Publishing

www.ingramcontent.com/pod-product-compliance
Lightning Source LLC
Chambersburg PA
CBHW070351220526
45467CB00001B/340